Long Road to
FREEDOM

The riveting story of a young boy
who lived under Communism in Russia

GOD BLESS YOU !!!

JACOB BRAUN

LONG ROAD TO FREEDOM

Unless otherwise indicated, all Scripture quotations are taken from the New American Standard Bible®. Copyright © 1960, 1962, 1963, 1968, 1971, 1972, 1973, 1975, 1977, 1995 by The Lockman Foundation. Used by permission. Scripture quotations marked (NIRV) are taken from the Holy Bible, New International Reader's Version®. Copyright © 1996, 1998 Biblica. All rights reserved throughout the world. Used by permission of Biblica.

ISBN: 978-1-77069-307-4

Printed in Canada.

Word Alive Press
131 Cordite Road, Winnipeg, MB R3W 1S1
www.wordalivepress.ca

Library and Archives Canada Cataloguing in Publication

Braun, Jacob, 1927-
    Long road to freedom / Jacob Braun.

ISBN 978-1-77069-307-4

    1. Braun, Jacob, 1927- --Childhood and youth. 2. World War, 1939-1945--Personal narratives, German. 3. World War, 1939-1945--Germany. 4. Immigrants--Canada--Biography. 5. Germans--Canada--Biography. 6. German Canadians--Ontario--Biography. 7. Ontario--Biography. I. Title.

D811.5.B73 2011   940.54'8243092   C2011-904964-3

Dedication

I dedicate this book to my good wife Kaethe, to my son Walter, to my son Siegfried, his wife Karen and their children (Alastair, Audra, and Adrianna), and to my son Peter, his wife Kathy and their children (Jessica, Bennett, Sydney Grace, and Nathan).

Contents

Acknowledgments

I would like to give special thanks to the following people: Dr. Timothy Sawicki, Ed.D, who is an associate professor and Director of the Online Physical Education Master's program at Canisius College in Buffalo, New York. He is a former neighbour who spent time on the manuscript without accepting any reward for his efforts.

Thank you to Peter Durksen, B.A., M.Ed, who is Kaethe's cousin and a retired school principal, for the time he spent improving the manuscript.

A special thank you to my friend Hans Kasdorf, D.Th, D.Miss, whom I first met in 1950. He has read my manuscript, and upon my request has been open and honest about my writing. He scribbled many suggestions in the margins and gave criticism where needed.

Our youngest son Peter, B.A., MACC (Master of Arts in Christian Counselling), spent many dedicated hours on this project.

Special thanks to Fern Boldt, M.Div., who has faithfully and patiently edited the manuscript. She is one of the most kind, supportive and encouraging persons I have ever met. She has worked tirelessly. We have exchanged countless emails. On several occasions we spent time in each other's homes to discuss important issues. We also appreciate Peter Boldt's helpful suggestions and for allowing Fern to spend time working on the book, rather than golfing with him. For this, both Kaethe and I want to express our sincere thanks and appreciation.

Thank you to Caroline Schmidt from Word Alive Press for coaching us through the publishing process. And special thanks to Evan Braun, editor extraordinaire!

Preface

I would like to give credit to a number of people who inspired me to write this book. My dear wife Kaethe and I have now shared more than fifty years of our lives together. We have often swapped childhood stories with each other, talking about our lives before we married.

Approximately forty years ago, Kaethe suggested that I write a book about my life. Almost like a vague dream deep inside, I felt that I had something to share with others. Yet it never entered my mind to write a book. Even if Kaethe had mentioned it fifteen or twenty times, it probably would never have registered with me. Besides, I had no time to write, since I was so involved in my trade as a cabinetmaker and looking after the financial needs of my growing family.

However, Kaethe doesn't give up easily. About thirty years ago, I finally started to write by hand. After writing twenty-five to thirty pages, I realized it would be a huge undertaking; therefore, it stayed in my drawer for decades. After I learned how to use the computer, Kaethe continued to badger me. She said, "Pick up where you left off." Now that I had time to write, I gave it another try. Without Kaethe's continued encouragement and suggestions, this book would probably never have been written.

Since I am a very private person, I waited until I had written a good portion before mustering up the courage to ask several friends to read and evaluate it. To my surprise, they encouraged me to keep writing.

Foreword

Every person has a life story, and each person's life is influenced by various factors. In Jake Braun's case, the predominant factors were his parents, world events, and his own interpretation of those events. Most people want to share their lives and stories with others, and in this Jake is no exception. Jake's story is particularly interesting because it takes place on two continents, under three political systems, and in the theatre of World War II, one of the most significant events of modern history.

Over the years, Jake has had the opportunity to revisit the places and people whom he encountered earlier in his life. This has enabled him to reflect deeply on his journey. Out of these reflections have come his convictions about the important things in life: family, biblical teaching, and perseverance. These values are evident from the first page to the last.

While the general format of Jake's story is chronological, it should be read as a series of conversations one might have with a good friend. All have great meaning for Jake, his family, and his friends.

– Peter Durksen

(Kaethe's cousin)

Every person has a story that can become known only when told. The many events and experiences—be they positive or negative—that have formed, shaped, and moulded our lives will remain hidden, unless we remove the coverings so that our fellow pilgrims can become acquainted with our stories. That is precisely what Jake Braun has tried to do in his story. He has made himself vulnerable, thereby affording a circle of readers beyond his immediate family the privilege of getting to know him in a personal way.

His emphasis is on events and experiences that make up the essence and content of the story. He has compressed into a minimal number of pages a lifespan of more than eighty years that stretch geographically from the Mennonite village of Neuendorf in the Ukraine to the towns and cities of Ontario, Canada. That is where our paths crossed for the first time in 1950, laying the groundwork for our continued friendship.

Jake's innate sense of curiosity, enhanced by a creative mind and wholesome ambition, are anchored in a deep faith in God, the Father of our Lord Jesus Christ. Therein lies the spiritual foundation of his life, which he credits to his early upbringing by devout and godly parents. Such are among the sterling qualities that have sustained him in times of poverty and deprivation. They have steeled him through the pain of separation from family and friends followed by months—if not years—of life in the German Army and the horrors of war. They have helped him endure ridicule, hunger, frost, and other forms of in-describable suffering in Western prison camps. He has lived through all of that—and much, much more—with-out forfeiting his wholesome sense of humour. There will be occasions for readers to wipe tears from their eyes, and times when smiles will cheer their day.

Jake tells of his life's vocation as a skilled carpen-ter, of his marriage to a Christian woman from a foreign land, of their life together as a family, of God's boundless providence and provision even when pain and sadness crossed the threshold of their home.

As I reflect on their story, I am moved to commend Jake and Kaethe for their ministry through song and music, especially to the elderly in church and community. The Lord never fails to reward kind acts of faithful service.

– Hans Kasdorf
(July 27, 1928 – March 26, 2011)
Fresno, California

CHAPTER 1

Life Under Communist Control

We lived with the never-ending terror of impending doom. Starvation stalked us in the early 1930s. The winters chilled us to the bone, as heating material was scarce. Even more nerve-racking, women expected a knock on the door or window in the middle of the night from a representative of the KGB, demanding her husband to come with them. They would say it was only for a few days, but everyone knew they would likely never see him again. He would be exiled to Siberia, where he would work as a slave in a labour camp.

Even though my mother was a deeply devoted Christian, she expressed her fears that this could happen to her husband and the father of her children. She feared to look one of those K.G.B. thugs in the face in the dark of the night. Therefore, we made curtains out of newspapers, because that was all we could afford. Would they take my father away? Thoughts of hatred raced through my mind towards the Communists, that demonic system.

Before the revolution, each farmer owned roughly fifty hectares (150 acres) of land on which he grew wheat and other grains. The Communists took away everything, except about a third of an acre, a plot of land where our house stood and on which we were allowed to plant anything we wanted. Naturally, we planted whatever was most important for the survival of our family, such as potatoes, carrots, beets, cucumbers, tomatoes, and spices. We also had apricot and pear trees and some currant bushes.

Soon, even from this small piece of land, they forced us to deliver a large portion of the potato harvest to the government. While I don't recall what the amount was, I clearly remember they had to be graded, and they accepted nothing but the best. If the potatoes were too small, they were rejected; we needed to come up with something better. An inspector came around every year to see what everyone was planting. The owner had to deliver a certain number of kilograms of the crop to the government, according to the size of the plot. It didn't matter if the family consisted of two, three, or ten.

Therefore, a smaller family with two or three workers was much better off.

The Communists not only wanted our potatoes, but they also came to see how many chickens and pigs we owned. They permitted each family to have one cow. A family of ten or more could surely use all the milk one animal could produce, but that wasn't how the government saw it. Instead, every family had to deliver a certain number of litres of milk to the system, regardless of the size of the family or the amount of milk their cow produced.

I vividly recall, as a twelve-year-old, carrying litres of milk to a designated place in the village. My mother, a deeply honest and conscientious person, would measure the milk every morning with a container made by the system, then add a little more to be sure it was at least the required amount. However, according to their measure, it was always too little. We carried a booklet with us for them to mark down the amount received. It always registered less than what we knew it actually was. They did pay us for the milk we delivered to the system, but it was next to nothing—an insult. However, if we purchased skim milk from the dairy, they always gave us less than what we paid for.

On at least one occasion, we had a cow that didn't even produce the amount of milk they required us to deliver. Consequently, we had to buy the missing amount and give it to them, leaving nothing for the family. Since this didn't make any sense, my parents did away with the cow. (I think we killed it and ate the meat.) Instead, we bought a couple of goats, because the Communists didn't want goat milk. We could have that for our family.

Also known as the Bolsheviks, the Communists didn't miss out on anything. They knew goats had fine wool under their outer layer of hair. To collect this wool, we had to comb the goat and strip it off the comb. We had to deliver a certain number of grams of this to the system every year. The same applied to meat and eggs. If we had one pig, we had to deliver a set number of kilograms of meat each year; if two, it would be more. They inspected how many chickens we had and ordered us to deliver dozens of eggs each year.

As you can imagine, having a cup of milk for ourselves was a rare occasion. Sometimes, after mother finished milking our cow, we would get a small amount to drink. It had to be a special occasion to have meat or eggs on the table. Once a year, around Easter, my parents tried to give us as many eggs as we wanted to eat.

Besides taking so many of our products and the small harvest from our personal plot of land, the Communists laid a heavy burden of taxes on each worker and homeowner. I remember the consequences of such taxation, especially from 1930–1938, when at times we didn't have a slice of bread in the house for as long as three months!

I had heard my parents talk about drinking real coffee before the Communists took over, but during my time, we only drank black coffee made from roasted barley. For breakfast, Mother baked small cakes made of sugar beets mixed with a little bran. Anything was better than nothing. Years later, she reminded us of those days. She said her heart had almost broken when we children stood around the stove and asked with weak voices, "Are the cakes almost done?" We often went to bed hungry. It was difficult to go to school and perform well in class on an empty stomach. One time a girl, whose parents were better off than many of us, had some compassion on me and gave me a good-sized sandwich. I have never forgotten that. If I knew of her whereabouts today, I would still thank her.

The government closed one church after another. The one in our village was converted to a storage building for grain. Therefore, we no longer had opportunity to go to church or Sunday school to learn about God. We only learned what our parents taught us.

Because there were no church services of any kind, there was also no such thing as celebrating Christmas or Easter. However, New Year's was always a great celebration. We were told that Communist spies lurked around after dark during the Christmas season, looking through the windows to see if our people were celebrating Christmas. Whenever they found someone doing so, they exiled the father to Siberia. My parents decided to celebrate Christmas on New Year's Day. This way they didn't rob us of the spirit of Christmas.

They constantly bombarded and brainwashed us with anti-God philosophy in school. Even the national anthem of the Soviet Union, which we learned to sing in both German and Russian, reinforced atheistic thinking. Here is part of it:

>*Wach auf Verdammter dieser Erde...*
>*Es rettet uns kein hoeheres Wesen,*
>*Kein Gott, kein Kaiser, noch Tribun...*

>(Wake up, you damned of the earth...
>There is no higher being,
>No God, no Emperor, no tribune to rescue us...)

The pressure to conform was especially powerful once we reached the third and fourth grades. The teachers told us stories about Lenin and Stalin's utopian dreams. After listening to these "sermons," sometimes from teachers who didn't believe what they were telling us themselves, they expected us to join the Pioneers. Joining this group was the first step in brainwashing people to become Communists. If we joined, we received a red tie with a shiny gold buckle, which I thought looked mighty sharp. In my class of about thirty students, only two or three didn't join; I was one of them.

Those of us who didn't join were kept after class so that the teacher could tell us more stories about Lenin and Stalin. Once she asked, "Now, aren't these nice stories?"

I answered, "Yes."

That was one of the biggest lies I ever told. I knew what I was expected to say, but just the same, I never did join the Pioneers. I knew too much of what my parents, especially my mother, had told me about her faith. She had also told us many stories and truths from the Bible. I didn't believe anything those Communists were telling us.

My grade four class. I'm fourth from the left in the dark shirt.

Not only did the teachers pressure us in school to go down the path toward becoming a Communist, they also came to our homes and tried to talk our parents into persuading us to join their ranks. I recall seeing my mother with tears in her eyes saying to one of these teachers, "We want our children to pray." Upon hearing this, the teacher responded, "They may pray at home, as long as they don't pray in school."

Economically, life was extremely difficult after the Communists took over. After they confiscated all the horses and farm equipment from the villagers, they started to tear down the farmers' barns, using the building material for their own projects. As far as I know, no one ever received payment for anything the Communists took.

Our barn, which was attached to the house, had an extension for storing hay and straw. When my father realized what was happening, he tore down and sold that storage area to enable one of the villagers to build a house for his family. It turned out to be a wise move, because it gave the Communists less to steal! They did, however, rob us of many other possessions.

My father worked about ten hours a day in a large carpentry shop. After coming home, he would continue to work at his workbench, placed in one of the three rooms we lived in. Since most people couldn't afford shoes, my father made wooden ones for most of the villagers. They were different, though, from the Dutch *Klompen*. The ones my father made looked like a slipper with a wooden sole four centimetres thick, so it would last longer. He made the front portion of the shoe from leather. He also made many brushes, mostly to clean horses at the *Kolkhoz*, the collective farms.

My father realized early on that I had an interest in and talent for woodworking. I started to help him around the age of ten. After I became more proficient at it, he paid me a small amount of money for my work. I once bought a chunk of bread in the village store with my earnings; another time I bought some sugar cubes. I bought woodscrews one day, even though I had no use for them at the time. If I had a ruble or two, I knew I had better spend it while something was available on the store shelves, which was not often.

Besides wooden shoes and brushes, we also used hard maple wood to make combs and acacia wood to make knitting needles, which were not available in the store. The needles were approximately twenty-five centimetres long. The women used them to knit scarves, sweaters, and other items. I also made wooden crochet hooks from acacia wood, which was strong and flexible. By making and selling these things, we earned a little extra income.

Since the stores had little clothing or footwear, we could seldom buy anything, even if we did have the money. Whenever it was announced that some merchandise had arrived, people would go to the store early in the morning while it was still dark and stand in line. It was difficult for someone in the middle of the line to get out, because everyone was pressed together. Once I stood in line while people pushed and shoved all around me. Suddenly, a Russian lady from our village jumped up and propelled herself forward on the heads of the crowd. This had happened before, but it was the only time I witnessed it firsthand.

When the store finally opened, the first customers were allowed to buy as much as their money permitted. Most of the others, who had also stood in line for hours, went home empty-handed, because there was nothing left to buy.

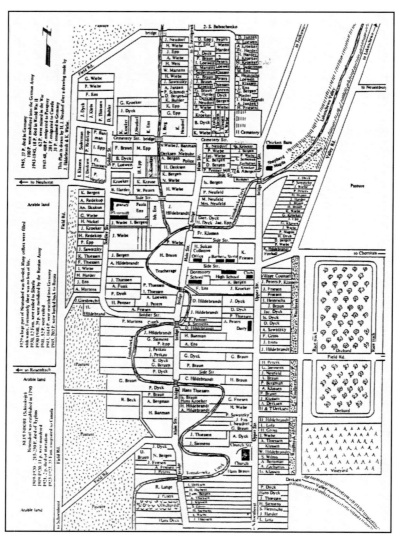

The Village of Neuendorf where I grew up.

CHAPTER 2

My Home and Family

I was born in the Mennonite village of Neuendorf in southern Ukraine. It was located thirty kilometres west of Zaporozhye and had a population of about fifteen hundred to two thousand people. Between Zaporozhye and Neuendorf lay the town of Chortitza, which was famous in Mennonite circles for its giant oak tree.

My parents were deeply devoted Christians. They demonstrated to us, by both their walk and talk, how to live a Christian life. All who knew them recognized their genuine and untarnished Christian testimony. I heard many positive comments and testimonials about them, even decades later, often from unexpected sources. I recall going to church with my mother at the age of five or six, but that changed as Communist control tightened.

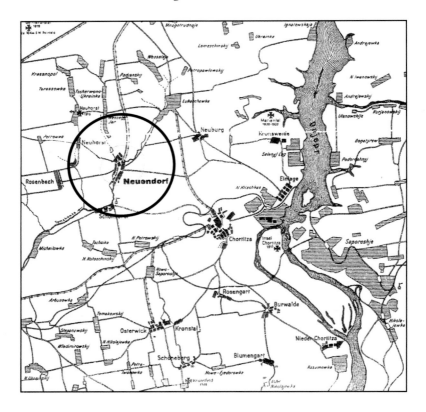

Where I grew up.

My father, Franz Braun, was born on September 10, 1903. My mother, Margareta, was born January 30, 1904. I had four sisters and three brothers. My oldest sister Susanna was born June 28, 1926. I was born on August 8, 1927. Franz joined the family on July 27, 1928. My sister Margareta arrived on September 21, 1930. Elisabeth came a year after that on November 26, 1931. Tina was born on October 10, 1934. Peter arrived almost two years later on July 15, 1936. My youngest brother Johann was born the next year on November 20, 1937.

Under such dire circumstances, imagine what it must have been like for my mother with a family of eight children. She also cared for my father's bedridden aunt for six years. In addition to the housework, my mother was forced to work on the collective farm in the heat of the summer. She loved to work, but because of all the fieldwork and the lack of proper food, she was often not well. Yet there was no mercy. She had to go or fear the consequences. When we children turned twelve or thirteen, we had to work on the collective farm during the months of June, July, and August, when there was no school.

Margaret, Jacob, Mother holding Hans, Susanna (back), Tina (front), Father holding Peter, Franz and Elizabeth

In the winter, Mother stayed home most of the time, but there was never a lack of work. She darned the family's socks, patched our clothing, washed and cleaned up, spun yarn from sheep wool, or knitted socks for someone. In fact, she made all our clothing, including our underwear.

We lived in a small eight-hundred-square-foot house. It had two large rooms, one small room, a storage room with shelves, and a kitchen with an open chimney, where the rain and snow blew in. Our family of ten, plus my father's crippled aunt, lived in these three rooms.

During the winter, it was always cold in the kitchen. The winters were brutally cold with a lot of snow. The temperature frequently dropped to -20 to -30 degrees Celsius. Sometimes it even fell as low as -40. Because the windows had such a thick layer of frost on them, we couldn't even see through them. A layer of ice at least an inch thick lay near the bottom of the windowpane. The snow banks outside were nearly a metre high. When the snow blew, it sometimes piled up to the ridge of the roof of some houses.

Father, the only breadwinner, worked for the Bolsheviks in a carpentry shop. He did fine woodworking. He could make almost anything from wood. His work was his art! I recall seeing a violin hanging on the wall which he had made with only a jack knife while he was in the Russian forestry service. In the late 1930s, he made an oak workbench that looked like an elegant piece of furniture.

Our house, as it appeared in about 1970. When I lived there, it had a thatched roof.

CHAPTER 3

The Influence of My Christian Parents

In spite of all these almost insurmountable difficulties, I clearly recall an atmosphere of peace and love in our home, because my parents trusted the Lord. When my father returned home from the shop, our parents often sang together after supper; my mother sang soprano and my father deep bass. I'm sure there was more contentment and peace in our home than in the mansions of many North American millionaires. We recently read in our morning devotional, "You don't need *more* to be thankful, but you need to be more *thankful.*"

We had many good times at home, in school, and with some of the neighbours' children. One of my earliest memories as a child of five or six was going with my mother to the field to take lunch to my father. I asked her, "How many languages are there in the world?" She named several, English being one of them. Somehow, this stuck with me; I always had an interest in English. The fact that three of my mother's sisters had immigrated to Canada about seven years earlier might have had something to do with that.

I often sat on my father's lap. He loved to play all kinds of games with me. Sometimes he had something in his hands or in one of his pockets that made a squeaky sound. I tried my utmost to find it by searching through the pocket I thought it was in, but he had already moved it somewhere else. Finally, he would reveal the secret. At times, it was no more than a squeaky pair of pliers needing a drop of oil.

Once he held a mirror in one hand and an apple in the other. He asked me to take the apple. When I tried to do so, he said, "Not this one, but the one in the mirror." We both enjoyed the many different gags he came up with.

He also had fun with my siblings. We played hide and seek indoors in the winter and outdoors in summer. He came up with ingenious hiding places. He also gave me piggyback rides in the summer by bouncing me around in the garden on his shoulders, making it feel as if we were on a bumpy road. Before we sold the barn, we always had a huge swing. The ropes were tied high up in the rafters and fastened at the bottom to a board for four or five children to sit on. He also put up some poles with string between them for high jumping.

Honesty, trustworthiness, and dependability were of utmost importance to my parents. They taught us these virtues by way of instruction, as well as by the way they lived. They said, "When you make a commitment, you must also keep it." My mother quoted Scriptures, such as James 5:12 (*"Your yes is to be yes, and your no, no"*) and Psalm 116:14 (*"I shall pay my vows to the Lord"*).

My sister Susanna was a year older than I, and my brother Franz was a year younger. When we were in our early teens, our parents allowed us to visit our beloved grandparents (Mother's foster parents), Peter and Margareta Siemens, and their sons Heinrich and Kornelius, who were close to our age. They lived about ten kilometres from us in Chortitza. We would get up early in the morning before sunrise, because it was a two-hour journey. We travelled by foot, of course, since we had no public transportation. Before we left home, my father told us to leave for home no later than 4:00 in the afternoon. That meant we had to leave at 4:00—not 4:05!

We had so much fun with the boys at Grandma's place, but we were careful to keep track of the time. Of course, we never owned a watch, but Grandma had a primitive wall clock. When it was close to 4:00, we asked again and again what time it was, making sure we wouldn't leave one minute before, but also not one minute after. Grandma was amazed to see us respecting our father's order.

Am I trying to make my parents appear perfect? Not really. I do recall thinking as a young boy, *If I ever have children, I will do some things differently.* I don't blame my parents or hold anything against them, but I want my children and grandchildren to have a realistic picture of the home in which I grew up. As all boys do, I misbehaved from time to time. Because Father was always on the job, it became Mother's responsibility to discipline us when necessary. However, she didn't like to use the strap, and when she did, it didn't hurt very much. When she spanked my younger brother Franz, he would turn around and say, *"Nah, waut kjielst?"* ("Hey you, why do you clobber me?")

There were times when she couldn't get our attention and said to us, "I'll tell your father when he comes home." In times like these, we were afraid to meet Father when he returned from work, because we knew we wouldn't soon forget what was about to happen. I decided that if I ever had a family, I wouldn't do this, and I didn't.

Here's a second thing I didn't agree with in my parent's home: my father wouldn't allow us to play with fire. It was actually a good rule, because our mattresses consisted of straw covered with burlap, the kitchen stove was heated with it, the barn was full of it, and the roof was made of it. However, we boys were crazy about wanting to make fire. Some of my friends made their own cigarette lighters, because we couldn't buy any. I followed their example, made myself one, and used it in secret. I wished my dad would have given me some matches or a lighter and allowed me to make a fire. Again, I said to myself, *If I ever have my own boys, I will give them matches or a lighter so we can make a fire and have fun.* I sure did, and we all had lots of fun doing it!

CHAPTER 4

Visits with Grandparents

In 1938, when the political atmosphere with Germany became delicate, to say the least, the Communists changed our school system laws. Up to this point, all our subjects had been taught in the German language. From now on, everything would be in Russian and Ukrainian. I was eleven at the time, with an older sister of twelve and a younger brother of ten. We could hardly speak a word in either Russian or Ukrainian. This meant hard work in school, not only to learn two new languages, but also to pass all the other subjects, such as geography, botany, mathematics, algebra, and geometry.

It was a big load, and my father knew it. He spoke to us older children in particular and encouraged us to give it our best. He made us a promise: "If you pass this school year without having to do any *Sommerarbeit* (summer school), I'll take you to the zoo in Zaporozhye." The city of Zaporzhye was thirty kilometres away, a place we had never been to before. We had also never seen a zoo. It was exciting, to say the least, since we had heard so much about wild animals. Anything new fascinated me.

Fortunately, all three of us passed our grades without any problem, so off to the zoo we went. This meant we had to get up around four o'clock in the morning and walk twelve kilometres to catch the train in Chortitza. On the way to Zaporozhye, we crossed the Dnepr River on a mighty high bridge. I looked out the window and spotted something way down below. At first glance, it looked like a duck. I immediately shared my excitement with my father, who told me, "It's a small rowboat." Sure enough, the tiny dot that looked like the head of a duck was the head of a human being.

I'll never forget all those exotic creatures I saw at the zoo.

My mother had been orphaned at the age of six. After living for three years in numerous places, she was adopted and lived in Chortitza with her foster parents for the next nine years. Her foster mother was only seventeen years older than she. They had three sons, two of them a little older than I, and one a year younger.

We became good friends. We never addressed them as "Uncle," but their parents were always Grandma and Grandpa to us. They were the only grandparents we ever knew. My father's parents both died when he was only seventeen.

After we were a bit older, Susanna, Franz, and I were allowed to go to Grandma and Grandpa's all by ourselves. We would wake up early in the morning and walk on a dirt road for the first five or six kilometres. After that, it was an asphalt road where the cars whisked by at lightning speed. It was exciting to walk barefoot on this smooth surface and not have our feet sink into deep dirt or dust.

Our grandparents lived just a stone's throw from the railroad station. We found it so exciting to watch that heavy monster of a locomotive arrive with all that steam puffing and whistle blowing. My father told us that if we put a coin on the track and let the locomotive run over it, it would flatten it. In spite of the fact that we had few coins, we decided it was certainly worth a try. Sure enough, after the train rolled over our *kopecks* coins, they were as flat as pancakes!

Another fascinating site was a huge heap of scrap metal next to the railway station. There we found one treasure after another: nuts and bolts, steel tubes, all kinds of wire, and other things that would made the heart of any twelve-year-old "nut" rejoice. We made homemade guns from the steel tubes. We flattened one end and curled it closed. Next, we filed a little hole through it, about one inch away from the closed end. We then stripped the heads off a bunch of matches and put them into the tube. After that, we chewed up some newspaper, formed little balls, put them into the tube, and tightened it with a steel rod. Finally, we inserted a large nail. We fastened this tube to a wooden shaft, which looked like the stock of a rifle. When all this was finished, one of us would take aim at the roof of a neighbour's barn. The other would light a match and hold it close to the opening made with the file. It made a loud bang and the nail shot out like a bullet!

We also invented other gadgets, simply to hear them make an explosive sound. Such explosions were particularly exciting to make under a railroad tunnel not far from the station. It created a sound and an echo that called for a celebration.

As one might guess, the late 1930s were not as bad economically as the early 1930s. We had enough to eat and energy to spare for playing these all-boys games.

Sometimes it was also exciting to use Grandpa's tools. He worked in a machine shop and had a drill press at home. Every boy had to have a jackknife. I used Grandpa's tools to drill a hole through one end of the knife so I could attach a chain to fasten it to my pants.

Grandpa was also a good musician; he sang and played the guitar like no one else! We really enjoyed that. Music always intrigued me. While we had a guitar and a violin at home, we had no one to teach us how to play them. I made an attempt once or twice on my own, but it didn't seem like I would ever be successful.

CHAPTER 5

My Parents

My mother, who lost her parents at the age of six, had three sisters and two brothers. Her oldest sister Luise, who was seven years older, looked after her like a mother. Her oldest brother Wilhelm died young; I never met him. Her younger brother Johann, whom I still remember, didn't lead a good life. My mother prayed a lot for him, as he had an especially difficult time during the Communist era. One day he disappeared, never to be heard from again. Mother's three sisters Liese, Tina, and Anna immigrated to Canada in 1925, while the doors were still open to escape from Communism.

Before my mother was adopted at the age of nine, she was kicked around from one home to another. She told us about one of the places she lived at the age of six. She had to get up at five o'clock and milk two cows before going to school, because the cattle had to be taken to the pasture as early as possible.

She lived in another home, at the age of seven or eight, where the man of the house was often drunk. One day when he came home drunk and angry, he yelled at my mother in Low German, *"Nem dien Pack 'n schea die foat!"* ("Take your stuff and get lost!") She fled to her guardian for advice. At the age of nine, Peter and Margareta Siemens took her in as a foster child, where she lived until she was eighteen. Those were *not* pleasant years.

Although her foster father was a gentle person, her foster mother, the one she spent all day with, wasn't. When my mother told us about the hardships and abuse she experienced, however, I never sensed any anger, bitterness, or lack of forgiveness against this woman. In fact, she told us she had forgiven her for everything. Her foster mother also asked my mother to forgive her after she left home.

Mother said, "The reason I'm telling you this is because I want you to know what I experienced." I clearly recall her saying, *"Daut wea ne gode Schol fo me."* ("That was a good learning experience for me.") I want to have the same attitude my mother had.

The Bible says, *"All discipline for the moment seems not to be joyful, but sorrowful; yet to those who have been trained by it, afterwards it yields the peaceful fruit of righteousness"* (Hebrews 12:11). Discipline, however, is not to be confused with abuse. My mother told us that her foster mother was an angry, irritable person who was ready to use the rod of discipline in the most unreasonable manner. When my mother didn't finish an assigned job quickly enough, her foster mother would throw her to the floor and beat her in an inhumane way. This happened many times. Once before doing this, her foster mother said, "I've been looking forward to this for a long time!"

The next time my mother would do her work more quickly. When she reported that she had finished the job, her foster mother would say, *"Dit jing so schwind, dout hast du secha aufjeschwient!"* ("This went so quickly; you probably did a miserable job!") She couldn't please her.

Once when things had become extremely difficult, my mother went up to the attic, knelt down, and prayed. While on her knees, her foster mother, who had been looking for her, found her praying. She was stunned. This time her "mother" hadn't said an unkind word.

My mother's foster mother, Margareta Siemens.

When Mother turned eighteen, she told her foster parents that she wanted to leave and find a job. They wanted to keep her, but my mother left anyway and began to work at *Betanien* (Bethany), a home for orphans. She worked there until she married my father in 1924, at the age of twenty.

As far as we children were concerned, Grandma and Grandpa Siemens were the best. It was always a celebration when our parents allowed us to go to their house and play with their sons, our friends. I thought highly of them. I once said to my mother, "I think you were fortunate to be adopted into this family." However, when my mother told us her stories of abuse, I became emotional. Even now, seventy years later, I still cry when I think about it.

Things were difficult for my parents after they married. While some of our people, including my father, were still hoping for better times, he decided to stay where he believed God wanted him. He inherited his parents' house and farm, which may have been a factor for him staying. However, things soon became progressively worse.

My father and mother both had Christian parents. Father's parents, Franz and Susanna Braun, weren't rich, but they lived comfortably. Besides the farm, Grandpa operated a small business, owned a store for some time, and also bought and sold grain. Then difficult times started.

Along with the Bolshevik revolution in 1917, there also came the *Machnovze* (Anarchists), as they were called. These organized gangs brutalized, stole from, and killed those they believed guilty of misusing and abusing the poor during the time of the Russian Emperor. They killed many innocent people.

They severely beat and inflicted much pain on my paternal grandfather. As a result, he became bedridden for the rest of his life. At the end, he developed a severe case of hiccups, which caused the whole bed to shake. He died shortly thereafter at the age of fifty-three. His wife Susanna died a month later at the age of fifty-seven.

If my father were alive today, I would ask him, "Why did your mother die so young? Was she also abused by those thugs?" My father accepted Christ into his life when he was seventeen, shortly before his parents passed away. It was such a comfort to them.

My father at the age of ten with his parents,
Franz and Susanna Braun.

CHAPTER 6

Memories of My Childhood

I found almost everything around me to be of great interest. When I was outdoors on a windy day, around the age of four or five, I wondered what was the cause of it being windy. I noticed large trees swaying severely. When I asked my mother about this, she tried to explain it the best she could. I don't really remember what she told me, but it wasn't how I had explained it to myself. I thought surely the trees were the *cause* of it being windy. After all, I knew if someone whisked an object briskly in front of me, I could feel the air moving. Well, I've since learned differently.

I was also fascinated about speed. I had many questions: how fast can people or animals run? How fast can a motorcycle, a car, or an airplane go? I realized no matter how fast anything moved, it still took time to get from one place to another.

As all boys do, I loved toys; one of mine was a small mirror. At the age of about seven, my brother and I sat in the sun and zoomed the reflection of it all around. We would aim it at trees, at the neighbours' houses, or simply into empty space. I remember wondering if there was something that moved so fast that it would take no time at all to get from one place to another. I observed the beam of light from the mirror reflected instantly, no matter how far away I would aim it. I also noticed the beam of light always appeared to be a straight line.

A few years later, my father came home from work with an amazing fact. Someone in the shop with a scientific mind had said that the speed of light was so fast, it could travel seven times around the equator in only one second. As scientists tell us now, it's about seven and a half times—not too far off from that first revelation.

I was also fascinated about space, the sun with all its planets, the moon and stars, and especially the planet Mars. For as long as I can remember, people talked about going to Mars. I hoped it would happen during my lifetime.

In the summer, as I lay on the grass and watched the clouds moving in the sky, I asked questions like,

"How high are the clouds?" or "How many kilometres to where the sky meets the horizon?" Later on, I became interested in knowing what it would be like to be high up in space, looking down at the earth, and seeing the whole planet with the clouds and weather patterns. Much later, I saw this on television.

As a child, my mother taught me a few things about our universe. She told me how I could distinguish the waxing and waning of the moon. If I saw the moon in the form of a sickle, I would start to write the small letter "z" to signify *zunehmend*, or waxing, increasing in size. If it looked like the letter "c," then I knew it was *abnehmend*, or waning, decreasing in size. She told me a few more things about the universe, the Milky Way, the Big Dipper, and other constellations in the sky. She emphasized in these lessons how wonderfully God had created our world.

One day my father told me about one of the brightest stars, the North Star. He told me how I could find it among all the thousands of stars I could see with the naked eye. Here is how: "Find the Big Dipper. Locate what is referred to as the two rear wheels. Draw an imaginary straight line from one of the wheels to the other, going from left to right. Go past the right wheel four and a half times the distance between the hind wheels, and there it is." He told me how this could be helpful if I ever got lost.

Many years later, I was a recruit in the German Army. Thankfully, I never really became a soldier, but I had to take part in some activities. I was stationed as a helper at the artillery with the FLAK, or *Flugabwehrkanonen* (literally, the aircraft-defense guns). The barrels of the guns were aimed exactly north when pointing to zero on the instrument panel.

One day I suggested to the corporal in charge, "Why don't we check to see if that is truly the case?"

"How would you do that?" he asked.

I said, "Let's turn the gun barrel to zero on the instrument panel, look through it, and raise it until it reaches the North Star." I looked through it and there it was—dead centre! After that, he also looked at it through the barrel of the gun.

A few days later, the whole battalion assembled, along with a high-ranking officer. My corporal suddenly stood up in the presence of hundreds of soldiers and excitedly shared what he had learned from one of his recruits—how to look at the North Star through the barrel of a gun. While no one asked me to stand to my feet and be identified, I have to admit I felt a little taller than I really was. In fact, I still feel good about it today.

Stars and space have always fascinated me. In the 1950s, I purchased a book, *You and Science,* to read about the most interesting revelations and discoveries, how our universe functions with all its complexity. I learned there are billions of stars in one galaxy, and there are billions of galaxies in the universe. Incomprehensible! On one page, the author showed the moon revolving around the earth, the earth around the sun at 67,000 miles per hour, and the sun with all its nine planets racing through space at half a million miles per hour. All the billions of galaxies operate on this same principle, racing through space in an organized way. Awesome! What a great God we have! How could all this ever happen because of one "big bang?"

This reminds me of a scientist I once heard lecturing on the nature of the universe. Among other things, he said, "In six billion years, our sun will become a nova (which means it will burn out), and all life on earth will come to an end."

A lady in the crowd asked, "How many years, did you say?"

"Six billion," he replied.

She said, "Thank goodness. You scared me for a moment, because I thought you said six million!"

We had picket fences with posts spaced eight to ten feet apart, with crosspieces on the top and bottom.

Vertical staffs of wood spaced approximately one or two inches apart. One of the neighbourhood boys loved to run along the fence, rubbing a stick against it and listening to that "ta-ta-ta" sound it made. He said, "I'd like to move so fast that, when I hold a stick against the telephone poles, I would hear this same sound." Well, if he were still around, I'd like to tell him, "Listen pal, you're moving at the speed of at least 567,000 miles per hour, and you don't even notice it. It costs you nothing."

As a youngster, I loved to climb trees and telephone poles. We had numerous large trees on our property. The fruit trees were especially fun to climb when the fruit was ripe. One huge pear tree was at least thirty-five feet high. We needed a long ladder to reach the lowest branch. These pears were about the size of a small apricot, but mighty good. We also had other varieties of pears with much larger, delicious fruit.

We had three large acacia trees that were good for climbing. They bore clusters of sweet-smelling white blossoms in the spring before there was any fresh fruit. They looked like they were loaded with snow. The bees weren't the only ones going after those blossoms; we ate them with gusto! They were almost as sweet as honey. No wonder Acacia honey is the best you can buy. Of course, in those days, we were happy to eat almost anything.

It wouldn't be fair, nor would it be true, for me to say we had only misery during the time I was growing up. We did indeed have many wonderful and unforgettable experiences. I wouldn't want to stroke out even the most difficult ones, such as the early 1930s. It's worth remembering God's blessings of supplying enough to keep us alive.

Church services didn't exist in those difficult years. However, my parents would gather with other believers, often in our home, to have fellowship. Mother told us once that she had been fed spiritually as they read the Scriptures and shared one with another, but she had to repeatedly fight the thought, *Oba me hungat!* ("But I'm hungry!") Many actually died of starvation in those days.

Once someone entered our house with his head covered so as not to be identified. He dropped something off which we needed badly—food—then disappeared without saying a word. Since we often went for months without proper food, we appreciated this person's kindness.

I give credit to my father for having the wisdom and foresight to distribute our food appropriately. He took the bread for each day, put it on the scale, and measured out exact portions—so many grams for each family member. What did we put on the bread? Butter was definitely out. In fact, I recall having butter only a few times in all those years. Butter, as a rule, was sold to buy bread.

We never had jam in our house, but my mother accumulated cream to make butter. I was the one who turned the crank on the little butter churn. After churning a long time, as much as half a teaspoon of butter would ooze out between the crank and the hole. I then swiped it with a finger, put it on a small piece of bread, and consumed it with indescribable pleasure!

For several years, the *kolkhoz* (the collective farm) gave each worker a small piece of land on government property where he could plant watermelons and cantaloupes. The soil and climate were excellent for growing them. In fact, anything except citrus would grow in this part of the Ukraine. Because we had our own watermelons, we could make watermelon syrup. It made an excellent dip for whatever bread we had for breakfast. Unfortunately, the Communists soon wouldn't give us land to plant them; therefore, no more syrup.

We planted sugar beets on the little land we did have and ate those. My mother also made syrup from them. However, unlike the watermelon syrup, the beet syrup created a scratchy feeling in the back of my throat. We added some milk to it, which made it a little milder.

In those lean years, our parents allowed us to put only two tablespoons of milk into a cup of coffee.

We butchered a pig once a year—a truly festive occasion! Our main concern was the amount of lard this animal would produce. This was, for the most part, the only fat available for cooking or spreading on bread for breakfast. We also made sausages and ham. We hung them in the open chimney to smoke them, and then stored them in a cool place. Another special delicacy for breakfast was *Lewaworscht* and *Repspeae* (liver sausage and spare ribs.) We cooked the ribs directly in lard. My parents made sure we didn't devour it all at once.

We also made *Grieben* (bacon cracklings) by grinding the bacon in a mincemeat machine and cooking it until it was golden brown. After that, they poured it through a strainer and used it to fry potatoes or spread on a slice of bread. I remember those *Grieben* during the lean years, because my mother made *Wotamos* (water soup) for breakfast. She filled a pot with water, then made *Streusel* from a mixture of flour, water, a pinch of salt and two spoonfuls of Grieben. She served breakfast for a family of ten with this! I must confess, my stomach didn't feel much different after eating, because I had filled it mainly with water. That was all we had. While it wasn't enough to make us feel strong and full of energy, it did keep us alive.

Once, my mother gave a small bowl of two or three cups of cracklings to our neighbour lady for their family of four or five. The lady responded with surprise and thankfulness: *"Dit reackt ons uk aul fo twe dogh!"* ("This will last us for two whole days!") My mother almost flipped. Our family of ten would have stretched that amount for at least two weeks.

The *kolkhoz* also supplied each worker with some sunflower oil. However, they never considered the size of the family. Those families with a father and two or three adult children working did quite well. Those with large families like ours didn't. Fortunately, these years didn't last forever.

Starting around 1938, every family with eight or more children received two thousand rubles each year. That was a great help and things became considerably better. We had enough food to eat after that.

The local government rewarded workers for outstanding performance on their job. My father received recognition almost every year for being one of the best. They presented him with a small token of appreciation. One year they presented him with a boy's suit. Another time it was a little piglet, which became food for us the following winter. Once they gave him a beautiful tablecloth, which my parents sold to another family that was a little better off, in return for some food. (Actually, the lady who bought this tablecloth was a friend of my mother's. Many years later, when she and her husband immigrated to Canada, she brought it along and gave it to my wife and me. We still cherish it today, seventy years later.)

My father went to work every day carrying a large handbag, called a *Koscholka*. With the permission of the foreman, he filled it with small waste pieces of wood and shavings for our stove to keep the house warm in winter. We had no firewood, since the Bolsheviks had taken everything away. However, the *kolkhoz* delivered several loads of straw to each worker. We placed it in a neat pile outside and used it in the stove for cooking our daily food and for keeping us warm in the winter.

Of course, it wasn't nearly enough for the whole year, so every summer we made bricks from cattle manure. We spread it on the ground in a layer approximately fifteen centimetres thick. As children, we mixed it by walking in it and kneading it like dough for approximately twenty minutes. After this, we put it into forms the size of large bricks and placed them on the grass to dry. Every few days we turned them over or set them on edge until they were completely dry. We stored them in a dry place and used them in the winter as one would use coal. To light these, we first made a good fire with wood, then put them on top. They didn't last as long as real coal, though.

Heating materials were so scarce at times that some people resorted to burning their furniture to keep from freezing. I know of a painter who burned some of his paint to keep warm. Once or twice, my father bought what looked like coal dust. He poured water on it and stirred it until it stuck together. He put this on top of a wood-burning fire. It created more heat and lasted longer than those manure bricks, but not as long as real coal.

Caravans of gypsies came through our villages. Many were fortune-tellers and did palm readings. Of course, they wanted to be paid for this. Some of our people used their services. However, my parents didn't believe in stuff like that and warned us to stay away from it. My mother advised us, "If you encounter questionable situations, something you are not familiar with, stay away from it." I have never forgotten that and have applied this guideline many times in my life.

Most of the gypsies were not trustworthy people. They would steal laundry from the clothesline. Once, in the presence of my mother and me, one of those fellows reached into a cabinet and took out a chunk of meat without asking. My sometimes-timid mother took it out of his hand and put it back in the cupboard where it belonged!

I recall many good times with Mother. She didn't have the opportunity to acquire much education, but she loved to read. On winter evenings, we sat on a wooden bench against the warm brick oven. She told us many Bible and other educational stories. She had a way of sharing them that made them come alive. She told us how she became a Christian as a young girl and how we could experience the same. We anticipated this story time and never tired of listening to her. In summer, when she milked the cow, one of us held the tail to keep it from whipping her in the face while she told the most fascinating stories. We could never get enough.

In 1934, when I was seven, a group of women, my mother, and I walked to Chortitza and Rosenthal to visit relatives. It wasn't difficult for me on the way there, but about three quarters of the way home, I became tired. I started to complain, hoping we could sit down and rest. Instead, one of the women encouraged me to run ahead to the next telephone pole, sit down and rest. I tried that, but it seemed like only moments before they caught up with me. I did that several times, unsure if I would make it home. After walking for more than two hours, we finally arrived. All I wanted to do was rest!

I had an experience with my father, which I will never forget. He took Susanna, Franz, and me to a place out in the fields where wild damson plums grew. They were smaller than the domestic ones, but since we didn't have much to choose from, we went to get these. Since it was fall, and there had already been a light frost, they tasted especially sweet. However, what stayed with me all these years is the feeling of the three of us being together with my father. Often words cannot describe what one feels, and this was one of those times. Such peace! Such a sense of bonding! Whenever I think of those times, it brings back pleasant memories.

CHAPTER 7

Boys, Toys, School, and Adventures

Because we didn't have many toys to choose from, or enough money to buy them, we manufactured our own. In early spring, when the sap started to flow in the trees, we made whistles from a willow branch. We cut a piece several inches long and tapped it with the handle of a jackknife for a minute to make the bark slide off. Then we made the necessary cuts in the branch, as well as in the bark, and slipped it back on. You couldn't buy a better whistle!

We also loved to make slingshots. Almost any tree branch in the shape of a letter "Y" worked perfectly. We used a piece of rubber tire tube for the sling. For ammunition, we rolled clay into small balls. Once dry, we used them to shoot at the neighbour's chickens, which had never learned to stay home. Of course, we used these clay pellets on all kinds of targets. At times, one of these "bullets" even found its way through someone's window.

Another one of our favourite toys was a flying propeller, which we made from a piece of sheet metal. We took an empty spool from Mother's yarn, used a wooden dowel with a shoulder for the spool to rest on, and pounded two small nails into the top of the spool. We drilled two holes just off the centre of the metal propeller and slipped it on top. We wrapped a string around the spool fifteen to twenty times, then pulled on it as fast as we could. What fun it was to watch that thing fly. Of course, once we did that, we had no further control over the propeller. Sometimes it landed where we didn't intend. Once it hit one of my younger brothers just above the eye. I considered myself lucky that it didn't land one or two centimetres lower. Thank God!

Every boy loves balloons, but we had never heard of buying one in the store. If we wanted one, we had to wait until our family butchered a pig. We cleaned out the bladder, blew it full of air, and tied a string around the opening. Of course, it didn't float in the air, since there was no gas available to fill it. Another thing we loved to do after butchering a pig was to hang the tail on the back of one of our friends, or a teacher we weren't too fond of. If we weren't careful, we could get into trouble.

While we were taught at home to be respectful to everyone, especially to our teachers and other adults, there were times when I preferred boyish activities to my school responsibilities. I was not particularly fond of athletics, which was often the last period. One of my friends and I had other ideas. We left school, ran to a creek under a bridge, and experimented with explosives. At other times, we rolled cigarettes with newspaper and filled them with dry leaves. Not long after that, several artistic students drew a cartoon, which they hung on the wall for everyone to see. It showed my friend and me escaping from school by jumping out of the classroom window. We hadn't actually jumped out the window, but we *had* escaped.

I participated in some other things which I'm not proud of today. However, I didn't do anything outrageously disrespectful towards our teachers, thanks to my upbringing. I also give credit to the Soviet Regime for a school program designed for high achievement. (I learned later that finishing Grade Seven under the Soviets was equal to completing Grade Nine or Ten in Canada.) We certainly had qualified teachers.

I was never at the top of the class academically, but I passed every grade with more than satisfactory marks. Obviously, I liked some subjects more than others; geography was one of my favourites. I even liked mathematics and algebra, once someone made it clear enough to make sense.

We had to learn many poems by heart, first in German and later in Russian and Ukrainian. This was always fun for me; it usually didn't take me long to be able to recite them. I still remember many of them today.

History was not one of my favourite subjects. We had to learn about the Romans and Egyptians who lived thousands of years ago, which I thought was of little value. My teacher, Franz Froese, not only loved this subject, but also got excited about it; this helped make it come alive for me. I still remember some of his dramatizations, with the aid of a blackboard, where he described the methods the ancient Romans used in battle.

There were about thirty students in our class. Our desktops had hinges that allowed us to lift the part closest to our bodies, flip it, and come down with a bang. We loved to do this. Sometimes even the girls joined in, making a horrendous noise! On one of these occasions, one of us realized the door to the classroom opened just a crack. The teacher was still standing in the hallway, peeking in without saying a word. Gradually, as one after the other noticed him, the noise diminished. Soon there was complete silence in the classroom. Our teacher walked in with a smile on his face. He never said a word about it.

Everyone respected him. He had few discipline problems with his students. Once, as a historian, he suggested we ask our mathematics teacher a certain question about history. Obviously, our math teacher wouldn't have a clue about this subject. I'm not sure this was a good thing to do to his colleague, but he loved humour. I don't know if anyone ever did ask our math teacher that question.

While our math teacher might not have known much about history, he certainly knew his subject well. He taught mathematics, algebra, and geometry. However, he had a totally different personality and way of applying discipline. It was rumoured that he loved strong drink. Sometimes he would get drunk and do foolish things. Apparently, on one occasion, he had smashed a door in one of the village offices.

When a student misbehaved in class, he would become angry, get all red in his face, and shout at the top of his lungs. While addressing one of the boys in this manner, the boy stood to his feet, stretched out his arm, pointed his finger directly at the teacher, and replied disrespectfully in German, *"Du go lewa no de provlenije dere tweischlone!"* ("You'd better go to the village office and smash doors!") While we were only allowed to speak Russian in school, the teacher also understood German. He replied, *"Ja tebe ne tey, a, wy!"* ("To you I am not *thou*, but *you!*") He was referring to a form of respect in addressing an older person. The student and teacher continued to shout the same insult at each other for some time until it finally ended. Because the teachers were not allowed to use the strap, it was difficult for them to maintain discipline. They could only use the psychological approach.

While I loved geography in general, certain things particularly interested me. I was fascinated by the skyscrapers in New York and other great structures of architecture and design. I wanted to travel and see these for myself.

Not only did I want to see the world, I wanted to see *the free world!* Even as a twelve-year-old, I had heard enough from my parents to know what life was like before Communism. I knew things were better in the free world. Three of my mother's sisters had immigrated to Canada in 1925. We corresponded with them in the early 1930s until it became too risky, due to the political atmosphere. During those lean times before the ban, Mother's oldest sister Liese, who worked as a nurse in

Concordia Hospital in Winnipeg, sent us food parcels with rice and other basic items. What a big help!

No matter how much propaganda we had to listen to from the Communistic regime against capitalistic America, I didn't believe a word they told us. Instead, I clearly recall as a young boy lying outside on the grass, looking at the clouds and sky above, dreaming about someday living in a "free world." I clearly remember having thoughts like: *If I ever get out into the free world, I will tell everyone about this evil empire. I will let people know what Communism is like.*

We loved our grandparents, especially Grandpa, because he was a good singer and musician. He also told us humorous stories. One I have never forgotten goes like this:

A Mennonite villager had a Jewish neighbour, whom he didn't trust very much. One day this man came over to borrow an axe to chop some wood. The Mennonite thought, *If I do, I might not get it back.* However, since he was a neighbour, he loaned it to him. A short time later, the Jewish man returned the axe along with a small hatchet. The Mennonite was speechless, and asked, "Why?" The Jew replied, "Your axe had a little baby."

Soon after, the Jew came to borrow a large pot. This time the Mennonite loaned him what he asked for without hesitation. Before long the Jew returned the pot along with a smaller pot with the same explanation: "The pot had a little baby."

The Jew knew his Mennonite neighbour owned an expensive fur coat. As winter approached, he came a third time and asked to borrow it, because he needed it to keep warm on a trip. The Mennonite responded, "I'll gladly lend you my coat." The Jew took it, but failed to return it.

After a considerable length of time, the Mennonite decided to go to his neighbour to see why his expensive fur coat hadn't been returned. When he asked him, the Jew responded, "Oh, that coat has died!" Obviously, this seemed ridiculous, so he asked again for it. The Jew said, "When I borrowed the axe and the pot and returned both with a 'little baby,' you believed it without hesitation. Now I'm telling you the coat has died, and you don't want to believe me." The Mennonite never saw his coat again.

Life was interesting. Once, Susanna, Franz and I went to visit our grandparents and their sons. Food was scarce, but they were a little better off than our family. After a two-hour walk, the three of us arrived so hungry we could have devoured a camel. Only the oldest son was home, and he invited us in to eat. However, the only food on the table was a crust of bread with no more than three slices. He said to the three of us, *"Nu aet, an wan jie dout aula op aete!"* ("Go ahead and eat, even if you eat the whole thing.") I could have eaten more than twice that by myself!

On another occasion, our grandparents visited us with their two sons. My mother prepared the table, and in spite of the fact we were poor at the time, there was enough to satisfy us all. I have to laugh when I think of what Grandma said as we sat around the table. She looked at her two sons, about twelve to fifteen years of age, and said, *"So kinja, nu aet, hia ess!"* ("Children, now go ahead and eat. There's plenty here!") I have certainly never held this against her, even though we were all struggling. We loved them unconditionally and enjoyed our times together.

It was so much fun to go to Chortitza to see the train and that heap of scrap metal I mentioned earlier. One day I noticed a large water tap outdoors, close to the railroad station. I could just turn a small handle and out gushed a big stream of water. Our water supply in the villages came from a well; we had to draw up one pailful at a time. As a kid, I wondered what would happen if someone forgot to turn off that tap. I suddenly envisioned the whole town being flooded! However, I never heard of the town being flooded.

When I was about nine years old, we had a well nine metres deep. A wooden pail, or some other object, became stuck way down below the water level. My father tried his best to fish it out with a rope and a hook, but he just couldn't do it. He asked us boys for a volunteer to go down to the bottom of the well and bring the item up. I volunteered. My father fastened a rope to the middle of a piece of wood. Then I sat on it with the rope between my legs, as he lowered me to the bottom. I succeeded. It didn't take me long to dislodge this item and bring it up.

What impressed me most was what I saw when I looked up from the bottom of the well. This narrow vertical shaft appeared to be a kilometre long. I could see my father looking down. It looked like the blue sky was resting right on top of the well! Not long after this, one of our neighbours had the same problem in his well. Who would they call but me to help?

I became very good at making different items out of wood. I loved to make toys or other objects to surprise my brothers and sisters on special occasions, such as Christmas or birthdays.

I also developed an interest in pulling teeth—"milk teeth," that is. My siblings often asked me to pull one of theirs. As news spread, even some of the neighbour's kids came to have me pull their teeth. One of my father's elderly friends, a blacksmith, made me a pair of tongs for pulling teeth. I was surprised when he presented them to me as a gift.

I also liked pulling slivers out of someone's feet or hands. One day, one of my sisters had a large wooden splinter in her foot and asked me to take it out. I didn't have anything available but a needle, a knife, and a pair of pliers. In this case, the later seemed to be the right tool. She pleaded with me to pull it out very, very slowly. Since I didn't want to frighten her even more than she already was, I promised to do just that. When I had a good grip on the splinter with the pliers, I jerked that thing out with lightning speed. She gave me a puzzled look, because she didn't realize what had just happened; she didn't even have time to think about pain.

When I was about four years old, my younger brother and I had a quarrel. My father stepped in and said that each of us needed to ask the other for forgiveness. He guided my brother to ask me first, and I said, "Yes." Then I asked his forgiveness, and he said "No!" I laugh at that now; I'm not sure how genuine my response was either, but I knew what was expected of me.

Our neighbour's house across the street was north from ours. One day their teenage boys decided to have some fun with a mirror. They endlessly reflected the rays of the sun through the windows of our house. Finally, my father had enough of it and came up with a brilliant idea. He picked up the ray of light from the neighbour boys' mirror with his own and reflected it back into one of their windows where he knew these boys' grandparents were sitting. Within moments, the problem was resolved. Clever Dad! It never happened again.

Another time, we were doing homework in the evening. There was some light in the house, but no curtains or drapes. Several of the neighbour kids kept knocking on our windows and making disturbing noises. When my father finally had enough of it, he carefully slipped out with a whip in his hand. Within seconds this problem, too, was resolved.

I found a magnifying glass to be a fascinating toy. Of course, I couldn't buy one, but there was always a way to obtain one. I received mine from a friend who had removed it from a Russian flashlight. It worked best in bright sunlight. I could hold it about an inch or so away from my friend's neck as he sat in front of me in class. He wouldn't even notice it at first. He would hit the back of his neck, as if trying to swat a fly. He finally caught on when it started to sting or smelled like smoke. At this point, it was a good idea to seek shelter or prepare for defence. *Bubenstreiche!* (Boyish pranks!)

This magnifying glass was strong enough to light a cigarette or make a fire. One day, a friend and I stopped at a creek on our way to school. We rolled cigarettes with newspaper and dry leaves. All of a sudden, a man, a smoker himself, appeared and yelled, *"Junges, saul eck jund de noash foll heiwe?"* ("Boys, do you want me to warm up your rear end?") We knew this fellow, with his dark complexion and big moustache, would indeed be capable of carrying out what he had promised. We decided to waste no time and took off as quickly as possible, leaving the smoke behind!

For some reason, the neighbour kids liked to play at our house. We did indeed have a lot of fun with them, especially in the summer at dusk or even after dark. We had many trees, some shrubs, and a prickly hedge, which were ideal for playing hide and seek and other games.

One of our neighbour's girls, a year older than I, was quite a storyteller. However, she exaggerated beyond believability. Her father was a truck driver. There weren't many trucks in our village of fifteen hundred to two thousand people, so it was something special to see one. We seldom saw a passenger car, unless the KGB had come to pick up one of the fathers to send him to Siberia. Anyway, this neighbour girl proudly told us that the price of only the *key* to this truck was 25,000 rubles.

I suppose her father had held up the key for the truck and had said to some other young men, "This key costs 25,000 rubles," meaning the price of the entire vehicle.

During the early 1930s, meat and dairy products were scarce. For milk, we had goats, as I mentioned earlier. For meat, we went to a field infested with rodents, which ate the grain crops. One of these, a type of field mouse called *Suslikie*, or gofer, was about the size of a big rat. They lived in deep holes in the ground. We carried water from the nearest creek or puddle and poured it into the hole. Sometimes it required more than one pail to get one of these creatures to come out. When it did come to the surface, we quickly grabbed it by the throat, held it firmly, and threw it to the ground. This would usually knock it out. If not, we gave it another blow.

Killing *Suslikies* tired us out, since the water had to be carried from quite a distance. Once the day's job was done, we took them home, skinned them, and stretched the skins out to dry. Later we sold them for a few *kopecks*. Those Communists certainly didn't overpay us.

The meat of these rodents became food on the table. I can honestly say it was every bit as good as chicken. I recall my father saying, "These are cleaner creatures than chickens; their diet is nothing but pure grain." I had the feeling he said that to encourage himself and all of us to eat them. Under normal circumstances, they wouldn't be food for human consumption.

Life did become better by the late 1930s. The time came when we had enough bread and potatoes, as well as vegetables and fruit. In those days, it was special for us to have white bread and have enough to feed all of us. In the summer, my mother baked *Bultje* (white bread) outside in a clay oven with a steel door at the front. She heated it with either straw or brush. Mother's hand served as a thermometer for measuring the right temperature. She would stick her hand about fifty centimetres into the oven and know exactly when the temperature was right to slide those loaves in. After a short time, we could smell the mouth-watering aroma of fresh bread. When it came out, it was golden brown. It was difficult to wait for the first slice; the crust was always the best part.

Later on, we could even go to the store to buy bread to feed our sheep. They loved it. However, my father told us a strange thing: "If you take a bite of a piece of bread, then offer it to a sheep, it will refuse to eat it." As strange as that may sound, I found it to be true.

CHAPTER 8

World War II and German Occupation

Our living conditions had barely started to improve when something happened to put a damper on it. The political atmosphere with Germany became tense. Before long, there was talk of war against Germany.

While most families didn't have a radio, somehow the news spread. One day our neighbour walked over to our place and told my father that Germany had attacked Poland. World War II had begun! My father asked, *"Es werklich chrich?"* ("Is there really war?") That was September 1, 1939, a day the world will never forget.

We began to sense the hatred the Russian population had against anyone who was German. We were referred to as *Hitlerzey* (disciples of Hitler). In spite of the fact that our ancestors had lived in this part of the world since the 1780s, and had done a lot of good for the country, we now became its enemies.

Soon the German army attacked Russia. It didn't take long before the Russian army marched into our territory. The war was frightening, but we also looked forward to being delivered from Communism. While we didn't experience the worst as the German Army approached, it wasn't a fun time for anyone.

One night some of the Russian troops were stationed in our village. A Russian officer knocked on our door, came in, and spoke to my father. Facing anyone from the Communist system made for a stressful situation. However, they left our village without harming anyone.

Soon thousands of local Russians started fleeing east from the Germans. They drove herds of cattle through our villages, including hundreds of cows with overflowing udders. The ones driving the cattle stopped the herd and allowed us to milk them. They let us keep all the milk.

I must confess some of our Mennonite people weren't all that sympathetic towards the Russians. Most of them were poorer and less educated than we were. This shouldn't have been a reason for looking down on them, but rather loving and helping them. Once some of these young Russian men stayed in our house for the night. We discovered, to our surprise, that they were Christians. We immediately bonded with them. I wanted them to stay a little longer.

Not long after the German attack, we heard rumours of their army coming closer. Large convoys of Russian troops with military machinery drove through our village to meet them. Finally, one of the villagers announced that the German troops were about to arrive. The Russian authorities gave orders for all of us to pack and move *east*. They gave a wagon and horses to some of the teachers and office workers. The rest of us didn't receive any transportation.

Of course, we had no intention of going east. A group of about twenty to thirty families decided to go *west* instead. We didn't go far, only a couple of kilometres, and hid in a cornfield for several days. From time to time, some of the men went back to the village to check for further news and to get water and supplies.

One day, a man came with the announcement that the German troops had actually entered our village. That was the best news! We all went back to our homes, experiencing freedom for the first time.

However, the Russian people in neighbouring villages weren't excited at all. In fact, they were afraid of the

Germans. Some of these people came to our home and expressed concern, but my mother told them, "Don't be afraid. The Germans are good people."

While I didn't hear of the Germans brutalizing or killing Russians, they weren't kind or friendly towards them either. Many stories circulated of the German soldiers going into Russian villages and helping themselves to eggs, chickens, pigs, vegetables or fruit, and then redistributing some of it to us. One of our relatives in Chortitza told us that the Germans had opened a storehouse and invited the villagers to come and help themselves. Because our people were free to take home whatever they wanted, some of the Russians did the same. However, after they had walked for some distance, one of the German soldiers called them back and ordered them to drop everything they had taken. They went home empty-handed. We felt disappointed; it was unfair to treat these poor people like that.

Things got even worse. Not long after, we heard of a Mennonite woman in a neighbouring town who had married a Jewish man. Since he was Jewish, he had fled east, leaving his wife and small child behind. When the Germans found out this child had a Jewish father, they took him from his mother and poisoned him. While we could hardly believe this to be true, we soon realized such things were indeed happening.

About this time, we heard that German soldiers had shot and killed ten Jewish men just outside our village. I was working with a number of women in the field who decided to go and see these corpses after work. I went with them and witnessed a pile of dead and decaying bodies. Some men were stripping these corpses of any valuable items. It was too awful to describe any further details.

The memory of this stayed with me for a long time. I wished I had never gone to see this. I felt guilty, realizing how good the Germans were to us, while killing others who had done nothing to deserve it. However, we couldn't do anything about it.

For us as Germans and Mennonites, life became better. The local authorities and the villagers held meetings to find a way to untangle the Communist system from the collective way of farming. The goal was to give every family its own land and farm implements. This was no small task, since there weren't enough horses or machinery. The interim decision was to group several families together, giving each one its share of what was available. They would also get to farm individually, as they had done before the Communist regime.

We were all looking forward to a better future, in more ways than one. Once again we had horses in our own barn, as well a couple of oxen. We also had some farm machinery!

CHAPTER 9

Freedom of Religion and My Conversion

Freedom of religion was important to the Mennonite people. The village church, which had been used as a storage house for grain, once again became a house of worship. I will never forget when we went to church for the first time and sang that great hymn, *Grosser Gott, wir loben Dich* (Holy God, We Praise Thy Name). At first, it sounded a bit strange, since some of us had never been to church. It was overwhelming to be able to freely express what we believed. The authorities even reintroduced the subject of religion in school.

Our village was quite large, approximately three kilometres long from one end to the other. The church was two kilometres from our home. Distance may have been a reason, but some of the Christians from our area decided to meet at our home for Sunday morning worship. Few ordained ministers remained, as most of them had been sent to Siberia because of their faith. Therefore, my father was asked to be the leader.

I had been brought up in a Christian home with the most sincere parents, but for some reason I wasn't interested in hearing God's Word. I sat at the back with some friends. Sometimes we said disturbing things during worship time. However, this changed when my oldest sister and some of the other teenagers became Christians. My sister Susanna had never been a bad person before, but after her conversion I noticed a genuine change in her. I perceived that she had a hunger and a love for the Word of God. She had a changed attitude towards other people, including me.

I suddenly realized that the Spirit of God was working in my life, too. I didn't have a Bible, but my parents had given each of my siblings and me a New Testament.

Around the age of fourteen, I was herding cattle with several others from our village. One of these men had become a believer through the assistance of my parents. He was a married man with several small children. Although he was more than ten years older than I, he became a true friend. I would take my New Testament along to the field and read when I had time while the cattle were grazing.

Another young fellow who worked with me used to ridicule my faith and New Testament reading. That never offended me. I only wished he, too, would become as hungry for the bread of life as I was.

I had been instructed in the Scriptures from childhood and been told how to come to the assurance of salvation. God had made it so simple. I knew John 3:16 from memory. I believed it, yet I struggled. I desired to know for sure that Jesus had died for me and had forgiven me.

One day, as I was battling with this question, I went into a ravine near some bushes and prayed out loud to God. I asked Him to give me the assurance I had been searching for. I didn't hear any voices or anything out of the ordinary. I wasn't asking or expecting anything spectacular; I just wanted to know beyond a shadow of a doubt that Jesus had made me one of His children.

I don't remember the exact day, but during one of these times when I was reading my New Testament, my eyes fell on 1 John 2:2, where I read, *"He gave his life to pay for our sins. But he not only paid for our sins. He also paid for the sins of the whole world"* (NIRV). It was as if a light went on. I said to myself, "This *does* include me!" At fifteen, still wondering if I had understood correctly, I shared my experience with some of my Christian friends, including my oldest sister. As I expected, they all confirmed this to be genuine. They encouraged me not to allow the enemy to rob me of what God had shown me.

After my oldest sister became a believer, she wanted to be baptized. The ceremony took place in the Dnepr River near Chortitza, about eighteen kilometres from where we lived. This town had a larger congregation of believers. As a baptismal candidate, my sister had to give her testimony in front of the church. Only believers and members of the church were allowed to be present. I was desperate to hear these testimonies, because I wanted what they had. The meeting took place in one of the residences. As it was summertime, the windows were open. I stood on something so I could see and hear what they said. However, one of the men promptly told me that I wasn't permitted to listen in as a non-member.

After I accepted Christ into my life, things changed. The Word of God suddenly became alive. I had a love for other believers like never before. Christmas had a new meaning; it had always been a wonderful time, largely because of the gifts and sweets we received, but now it had an added dimension, a deep inner peace and joy that could only be fully understood if you have experienced it yourself. Our Sunday morning services and Saturday evening prayer meetings became more meaningful.

Other believers helped me along the way. It was our custom at prayer meetings to kneel down and pray audibly, if we wanted to. I felt the urge to take part in this open prayer, but resisted for a time. Finally, I confessed my faith in the Lord by praying in the presence of other believers. I'll never forget the victory I experienced as a result. My fear of others diminished; praying in public became easier. I will never regret having made this decision.

I have to confess what I have heard many others say, "How I wish I were able to say that from now on everything went well. I have always walked with the Lord and basked in his presence." However, this was not my experience. While I desired to do God's will, I soon realized I still had my old nature. The apostle Paul confessed, *"For the good that I want, I do not do, but I practice the very evil that I do not want. But if I am doing the very thing I do not want, I am no longer doing it, but sin which dwells in me"* (Romans 7:19–20). However, he also said, *"I can do all things through Him who strengthens me"* (Philippians 4:13). I thank the Lord that, in spite of my failures, He doesn't condemn me, but continues to lead and love me just the same.

Two years passed with German occupation. Economically, things slowly got better. We especially enjoyed the freedom to practice our spiritual convictions and faith. We continued having Sunday morning services and Saturday evening prayer meetings in our home. More and more people from our village came to these meetings and souls were being saved. People from neighbouring villages, even five to ten kilometres away, came by horse and wagon. Even some German soldiers attended. I can still remember how these men enthusiastically sang those wonderful hymns, glorifying the Lord and lifting our spirits.

Before long, some Russian believers from a neighbouring village came. I still remember Philip Schwatschka, the first one who attended. My parents referred to him as *De Rusche Broda* (the Russian brother). He was, indeed, a loving brother! My mother, one of my siblings, and I visited this "brother" at his home five or six kilometres away. They even served us a meal in their home.

On occasions such as Christmas, New Year's, and Easter, our small congregation put on special programs. Sometimes we also assembled in the village of Rosenthal, near Chortitza. They had a larger congregation with some outstanding speakers. They also had a large choir with a trained conductor. It was truly a joy to listen to them.

Shortly after the German troops occupied our area, they made specific plans for governing the new territory and decided who would be in charge. They chose two high-ranking German officials to govern the district, and they would be officially installed in Chortitza. A convoy of German automobiles with high-ranking officials would have a "march-past" down a beautifully paved highway five kilometres from our home. We made sure we didn't miss the occasion. When we arrived, we found thousands of people waiting along the highway to witness this first-time demonstration of pride, power, and majesty.

At first, what appeared to be military police arrived to secure the area. A few minutes later, the convoy started marching past. First, there were a number of highly polished and sparkling automobiles, such as we had never seen before. Inside them sat men dressed in immaculate, sharp-looking uniforms. Between each automobile marched five or six men abreast, about four or five deep. Some of these groups wore golden brown uniforms, others a dark navy blue. With sharp hats, shiny boots, and gleaming buttons and decorations, they marched perfectly. What a majestic sight! Nothing I've seen since even came close to this. To say this was impressive is an understatement. It was majestic! Everything was so brilliantly designed; you could get goosebumps as an onlooker.

CHAPTER 10

Goodbye, Ukraine; Hello, Germany

As time went on, so did the war. Nearly two years after the Germans came, we realized that the Russian troops were gaining the upper hand. As a result, we were ordered by the German military to pack up and make our way west to Germany. Fortunately, they allowed the people in our area to travel the seven-day journey to Poland by freight train. Obviously, we could only take a limited number of belongings with us. Even though we weren't rich, we sorely missed much of what we left behind.

Thousands of less fortunate German-speaking people had to travel by horse and wagon or oxen. This caused them much suffering and made their trip much longer. Although ours was a relatively easy evacuation, it was by no means a pleasure trip.

Each of the rail cars was packed full of people. In order for each person to lie down at night, some of the men constructed a platform five feet off the floor. One night, part of this platform gave way and toppled down on the ones sleeping underneath. One of the women received a broken collarbone. There were many other injuries.

We occasionally noticed German soldiers with rifles standing watch along the railroad for fear the enemy would put explosives on the track. A locomotive pushed several cars loaded with sand ahead of itself to minimize the damage in the event of an explosion. Whenever the train slowed to a snail's pace, we feared the worst.

We left our homes in the Ukraine on October 10, 1943 and arrived in Prussia, the Polish part of Germany, on October18, 1943. A large sign on a building at one of the railway stations read *"Gross Deutschland gruesst Euch!"* ("Germany the Great greets you!") In a city named Litzmanstadt (Lotz), we had to go through *Entlausung*, a process to get rid of lice. Each person had to take off all his or her clothing and take a hot shower. They sent the clothing through a heated oven. After this, they transported us to the city of Kulm an der Weichsel.

We lived in wooden barracks. Each room had a small coal-burning stove to keep us warm. They gave our family of ten a large room to live in. Smaller families received half a room. This didn't seem so bad. We had enough to eat, even though we didn't like the taste of some of the food, especially the soup. However, the Germans baked delicious bread. We especially liked their *Broetchen*, a large bun. I also liked their vanilla-flavoured pudding with an awesome strawberry or raspberry topping.

They didn't hesitate making us German citizens. One day, a fancy train arrived with all the necessary personnel and equipment to register us. By becoming citizens, we had the same privileges as well as responsibilities as any other German national.

While I was happy to escape from Communist Russia, I will never forget how homesick I was as a young teenager. I longed to be back home where I had grown up. I don't know how many times I was overcome with intense desires and cried by myself at night. Had it not been for the Communists, I would have given anything to go back home.

We were not forbidden from holding religious services, but they had a clever tactic for keeping us from going to church. Every Sunday morning they ordered us to line up for *Hitler Jugend Dienst* (Hitler Youth Service). When some of them found out we believed in going to church, they sneered at us and said, "Church is for old women."

They soon drafted any male eighteen and older into the army. If you were under eighteen, you automatically become a member of *Hitler Jugend* (Hitler Youth). They issued us appropriate uniforms and required us to attend *Hitler Jugend Dienst*. This also applied to the girls. Anything that had to do with church was out of the question for us young people.

Sometime in the summer of 1944, they transported our family to the village of Vogtsberg, in the area of Velun. Here we witnessed further mistreatment of the Polish people by the Germans. They ordered the residents and owners of the houses to move out and settle in barns. In our particular situation, the Poles were still moving their belongings out as we arrived to move in. None of us could do anything about that.

We had a small house on a sizeable lot with some vegetation. At first, we worked on a large farm owned by a German farmer. In July of 1944, my father was taken from our home to work in construction in another part of Germany. I never saw him again. He died years later in Russia on September 28, 1971. Not long after my father left, they took my younger brother and me to dig trenches to keep enemy tanks out of our territory.

Every morning we marched to work with a pick and shovel. The person at the front carried the German flag. We sang nearly all the way to work. One day I saw a local Polish farmer riding on a horse-drawn wagon. All of a sudden, one of our sixteen-year-old boys ran to his wagon, jumped up on it, grabbed the farmer's hat, and threw it away. Then he started to beat the driver left and right on the head. I was shocked, but I was too afraid to ask anyone about such brutal treatment. Not long after this incident, I witnessed the same thing again. This time I got up the courage to ask about it. I was told that it was because the man had not honoured the German flag by taking off his hat.

In Vogtsberg, the German authorities required us to wear swastikas on our shirts and jackets for identification purposes; the Polish residents had to wear a large letter "P." One day, as a seventeen-year-old, I went to the butcher shop. When I saw the long line-up, naturally I got behind the last person. There I witnessed one of the greatest acts of discrimination I've ever seen. When the clerk at the counter noticed the swastika on my jacket, she motioned for me to come forward and be served. The local residents had to wait, just because they were

Polish. I often wondered how the Germans could be so foolish and blind. They were supposedly the most enlightened and intelligent people on earth. Now, with almost the whole world against them in this war, how could they be so *dumb?*

If they were so determined to make slaves of everyone, why didn't they first make friends with them? Then they might have even helped fight the war. I wasn't surprised that so many were eager to harm them and stab them in the back during and after the war. I heard German people say, *"Das ist ein Wahnsinn!"* ("This is insanity!") Those who did attempt to stop this insanity were put to death—Dietrich Bonhoeffer, a German Lutheran pastor and theologian, was one of them.

During the time we lived in Poland, every male sixteen and older was repeatedly called to appear before a German military official. On one occasion, they pressured about fifty of us to join the military voluntarily. After that, they called us individually to appear before a high-ranking military officer who tried to persuade us. However, I was a Christian and had been brought up with the conviction to support life rather than to cause harm, least of all *kill*. I expressed my conviction and gave my reason for not volunteering as best as I knew how.

"I won't volunteer," I told him.

He said, "If you don't volunteer, you'll be drafted, and you'll have to join anyway."

"If I have to go, I suppose I'll go, but I won't go voluntarily."

"We want to be able to tell our opponent that our youth has volunteered one hundred percent to be part of the German army."

When he finally realized he was unable to persuade me, he put his hand on my shoulder and said, *"Dann gehen Sie in Gottes Namen!"* ("Well, then you go in the name of God!")

While religion and church attendance was not officially forbidden, the Germans did make mockery of it. We wouldn't even consider praying or saying grace before a meal. Instead, as about fifty of us teenagers sat in a circle on the ground, the officer in charge would ask a volunteer to recite a verse before eating. One of the teenagers would say the following: *"Zigaretten, Schnaps, und Wein sollen unsere Feinde sein, doch in der Bibel steht geschrieben, wir sollen unsere Feinde lieben. Allemann?"* The rest of them would shout, *"Ran!"* ("Cigarettes, whisky, and wine shall be our enemies, yet in the Bible it is written that we are to love our enemies. Everyone?" The rest would shout, "Dig in!")

CHAPTER 11

In the German Army

In the fall of 1944, I received a citation to appear at *Wehrertuechtigungslager* (military training camp), where I would prepare for battle. Here they instructed us in how to use a rifle, machine guns, hand grenades, and other weapons for destroying tanks. Towards the end of November, I received a draft order to appear in a certain city in Poland on December 15, 1944. When my mother realized I was about to leave, she said she had had a premonition recently while baking cookies for Christmas that they might be for someone in the family to take with them.

Early in the morning of December 15, the authorities ordered one of the Polish farmers to take me to the railroad station. My mother and sister Susanna came along.

This was the last time I saw my mother for thirty-six years! I wouldn't see her again until 1980, in Germany. When they left for home, I boarded the train for Shiraz.

From there, they took me to another centre where they outfitted me with a uniform, but I wasn't given a rifle or other weapon. I will never forget the apprehension I felt as we received one piece of clothing after another—underwear, socks, outerwear, and coat. Last of all, they gave me a steel helmet, which was a clear indication of what was to come.

The German authorities announced the day when we would be officially sworn in to become German soldiers. Since I was a Christian, I had learned in the Scriptures, *"But above all, my brethren, do not swear"* (James 5:12). I didn't want to participate in this ceremony, so I went to see the officer in charge. He invited me to his office where I stated my position regarding the oath. To my delight, he didn't try to persuade me to change my convictions. Instead, he asked numerous questions as to why I believed the way I did. He wanted to know where I was from, who my parents were, and about my Christian upbringing and heritage. When I told him I came from a Mennonite family, he was interested in knowing more about our people. That's when I told him we didn't believe it was right to say, "I swear." He said,

"Dann werden Sie morgen geloben." ("Then you will affirm tomorrow.") That meant I would make the same commitment to Adolf Hitler as the rest, except instead of saying, "I swear," I would say, "I affirm."

The swearing-in ceremony was impressive. They had invited a high-ranking military general to attend. The recruits all lined up outside; it was a bitterly cold day. After a brief speech, the recruits raised their right hands and repeated after the commanding officer: *"Ich schwoere bei Gott diesen heiligen Eid, dass der Fuehrer des Grossdeutschen Reiches, Adolf Hitler..."* ("I swear before God this sacred oath, that the leader of this Great German Empire, Adolph Hitler...") Then we were to promise to do whatever it took to be a faithful soldier, even unto death.

While the rest of the nearly one hundred recruits stood outside freezing, I alone was allowed to stay inside and keep warm by a coal-fired stove. Everyone noticed that I had not taken part in this ceremony. A number of them came to me later and asked, "What's going on with you?" This gave me another opportunity to testify what I believed. I was delighted when the day for me to "affirm" my commitment to the army never came!

They didn't send us directly into battle; instead, we traveled by rail from one place to another. One of the first stops was Konigsberg, where we stayed approximately ten days. It was a huge complex of military armouries called Immelmann Kaserne, close to the Baltic Sea. The buildings were clean and well-kept—a pleasant place to stay.

Two things impressed me there. One was the fantastic taste of coffee in the morning—black, with no sugar or cream. I had never tasted such good coffee. The second thing was the way we celebrated Christmas. They served us a delicious meal in a large room, giving us each a large bag filled with Christmas goodies. My first thought was to send part of these goodies home to my mother and siblings, who didn't have much during the war. I did send some of it. Unfortunately, I never heard of them receiving it.

While sitting around the tables after the meal, someone requested we sing some Christmas carols. We soon realized most of the recruits were either totally unfamiliar with them or had absolutely no interest in singing them. Therefore, someone suggested we sing some military songs instead. With this, the Christmas spirit came to a sad end.

I was thankful that I never really became a soldier. The training we received here and in the Hitler Youth bordered on tyranny. No one had any idea why all the harassment and bullying took place. They would order us to line up outside, and the commanding officer yelled, "Everyone lie down! Get up! Lie down! Get up! Lie down and move forward!" Then we pulled ourselves forward on our elbows until we were exhausted. Another favourite trick of theirs was to make us bend over, grab each heal with one of our hands, and move forward. This they called *Entenmarsch* (the duck walk). They tormented us until we almost dropped dead; they never gave a reason beforehand.

One rainy day, they made us crawl in the mud in our dress uniforms. When the officer finally ended this tyranny, he explained the reason for all the cruelty—one of the recruits had thrown a piece of bread into the weeds behind a barn. They justified it with this slogan: *"Eisner fuer alle und alle fuer einen."* ("One for all, and all for one.") If one person did something wrong, all had to receive the punishment. Because of this exercise, our uniforms were covered with mud. The officer commanded us to go to the barracks and clean up. He ordered us to be back within ten minutes with spotless uniforms. "They can be wet," he added.

At the end of December, we traveled to Oberschlesien. This time it was by freight car; was it ever cold! We stopped at one of the railroad stations to have something to eat. Since we used a wood-burning stove in the rail car and had straw on the floor to sleep on, two of the young recruits were ordered to stay behind to make sure it didn't catch fire. However, shortly thereafter someone yelled, "Our car is on fire!" We all rushed over. The two fellows who had been left to watch the stove threw some of the baggage out to spare it from burning. They rescued what they could, but the fire was so severe that they had to escape to save their own lives.

Every other mother had packed some special goodies into her son's suitcase, as also my mother had. Fortunately, my stuff was saved, but the belongings of a boy I grew up with were burned to ashes. I decided to share my goodies with him to minimize his loss, especially since it was the Christmas season.

Most of the time, we didn't know why we were traveling or what our destination might be. One of these times we found out the Russians had encircled us twice! Since we had no weapons, we were fleeing rather than defending. This wasn't as bad as being in frontline combat, but it was far from a vacation.

The Russians were constantly on our heels. We could no longer travel by rail, or even horse and wagon. They ordered us to pack up and march. We had two sets of horses to pull the wagons, which were loaded with as much stuff as they were able to carry. Except for the driver, everyone marched behind the wagons. The journey took two weeks—a distance of 240 kilometres. It was horrendous!

We spent one night in a large room sitting on chairs. Another time we slept on straw. Shortly after that, we discovered we were all infested with lice. Later we were told that Russian prisoners had spent the night before us on that same straw. Lice or no lice, we had to carry on.

One encouraging thing happened, though, whenever we went through the cities and villages. As soon as the inhabitants spotted us, they came and served us sandwiches, baked goods, coffee, and tea. Sometimes they threw packages from the second or third floor of buildings. A young woman came with a large platter filled with food. Several of our group rushed to her in an uncivilized manner. They were pushing and shoving, each one trying to get the most. I feared she might get injured, and she might have been. I was so embarrassed. People can be so much like wild animals.

One day on this two-week march, it was obvious that the Russians were just around the corner. The Germans gave us orders to drop everything at the side of the road, except the clothes on our backs. I suddenly realized my best pair of shoes was in my backpack. I was going to put them on and leave the worn ones behind. However, there was no time for this; we needed to run. They even threw the supplies on the wagon to the side of the road to lighten the load and avoid being captured. If we didn't want to fall into the hands of our worst enemy, we needed to keep going, even though we were dead tired. Those who were about to collapse were given time to rest on one of the wagons for a short time. I never received a turn.

In spite of my tiredness, I realized many people had suffered under worse conditions. I saw convoys of both young and old civilians fleeing from the Russians. Some had only a small hand wagon or loaded-down bicycle. Many were on foot, running as fast as possible. Having a motor vehicle was indeed a privilege, but even that could be a problem. I saw a small truck with one of its rear tires missing; it kept driving on the rim.

It was extremely cold while we marched—snow all over—an unforgettable sight! We once found a half-dead Russian soldier lying in the snow at the side of the road, crying out, *"Oj, Oj! Wosmitje menja!"* ("Oh, oh! Take me with you!") I don't know if anyone besides me understood what he was saying, as I was still fluent in Russian. When you see such situations, you don't need to understand the words. In spite of our own predicament,

I heard some of our recruits spewing insults and curses at the dying man. Obviously, we were not in a position to help him. However, had he been a German soldier, I'm sure our commanding officer would have said, "Let's put him on one of our wagons." War is horrible beyond description!

We continued our march until we arrived in Sudetenland, in Czechoslovakia. Many German-speaking people lived in that area. One evening we arrived in the town of Koenigswald. They placed each one of us in a private home. They assigned me to the home of Mr. and Mrs. Emil Hilsch, who had a lovely twelve-year-old daughter. They lived in a fine home with hot running water. These good people treated my clothing to get rid of the lice. I took a warm bath, which I hadn't had for a long time.

Before I left, Mrs. Hilsch gave me some food for the journey, including a whole jar of strawberry jam. I had never seen anything like this! Before I departed, the twelve-year-old girl gave me their mailing address. I intended to stay in contact with this family and wrote letters to them for many years. I also received lovely letters from this girl. I still have some of them. Eventually, we lost contact.

After marching almost day and night for two weeks, our journey finally ended. On Thursday, February 1, 1945, we traveled by train to the city of Halle, near Leipzig. After numerous stops, we arrived there on February 24, for further training. Their goal, of course, was to make soldiers out of us.

When we finally arrived in Halle, they placed us in *Eine Grosskampfbatterie* (a major military complex). Here they had twenty-seven huge 8.8-centimetre FLAK anti-aircraft guns cemented into the ground. They used this machinery to bring down as many planes as possible, as the "enemy" flew over Germany, bombing major cities, important industrial areas, and military installations such as ours. These guns were divided into groups of nine each. The guns were spaced about fifty metres apart. A wooden partition surrounded each gun, creating space for the gun operators. There were small rooms behind these partitions for ammunition.

One of these rooms was large enough for six or eight men to go inside to warm up during the orders to stop firing. It had a small coal-burning stove. There was a layer of concrete about four inches thick on top of the ammunition and a wooden partition separating it from the space where the men rested. Outside was a heap of dirt about five feet high to protect us from enemy fire.

Each gun required at least six men to operate. The officer in control received orders by phone from the main command station. One of the gun operators ("K1") sat on a seat with a steering wheel in front of him, which he turned according to orders given electronically. It had two dials, similar to a clock. Each dial had one hand guided electronically from a nearby underground location. The other hand moved as "K1" turned the wheel. Both dials were numbered from one to twelve. The responsibility of this individual was to match the movement of his "hand" to the electronic "hand," which often zoomed around like a bee from flower to flower. By turning the wheel, he raised the barrel of the gun up or down.

I, the "K2," had the very same responsibility, except turning my wheel moved the barrel of the gun either left or right. "K3" loaded the gun by taking one grenade at a time out of a "cup" that automatically adjusted the timing for the grenade to explode at a distance determined electronically. Besides these, we had a number of helpers—some of them German teenagers, others Russian prisoners of war. They forbade us from speaking to them. I have to confess, though, that since I was fluent in Russian, I did have some short conversations with them.

When the order to fire was given, a bell rang. "K3" pushed a grenade inside the huge barrel and pulled the trigger. All twenty-seven guns fired at the same time at the same target—an enemy plane. To prevent damage to our eardrums, they gave us earplugs and instructed us to open our mouth wide at the sound of the bell. That was indeed good advice, because the horrendous, thunderous explosive sound of all twenty-seven monsters firing at the same time was almost unbearable. We felt the earth tremble!

During the last few weeks of the war, enemy airplanes flew overhead day and night. Each time, we ran to our designated positions and took aim at these flying monsters. When the bell rang in our barracks in the middle of the night, we jumped out of bed, dressed with lightning speed and raced to our positions. There wasn't time to put our shoes on—only wooden slippers. On at least one night, we fired eighty shots from each of these guns.

As the American Army came closer and closer, our ammunition became scarce. When enemy planes flew overhead, we couldn't fire at them. One day American planes dropped hundreds, if not thousands, of bombs on the nearby city of Halle. We could see them falling. It looked like it was raining bombs! I had never seen anything like this before. The sound was indescribable; we couldn't distinguish one explosion from the other. It felt like it was the end of the world!

One day we were ordered to dig trenches near where we were stationed. All of a sudden, American airplanes flew overhead dropping thousands of leaflets addressing the German people. They attempted to persuade the public to stop resisting the Allies. They even suggested that the German people work against their military forces, by whatever method, to end the war as soon as possible. The pamphlets also included a threat. If Germany continued to resist, the Allies would attack so ferociously that not much of the country would be left. Our leaders forbade us from reading these leaflets. However, it was obvious that the end was near. After we picked up these leaflets, we went inside our *Mannschafts-bunker* (bunker), with the coal-burning stove. We didn't know what awaited us.

As it turned out, our installation became their next target. Minutes after these planes dropped the leaflets, they returned—not with leaflets, but with bombs. I never stared death in the face closer than in those moments! As soon as we heard the crashing, thunderous explosions of bombs all around us, we laid flat down on the brick floor. The bombs dropped right on top of us. The earth trembled! The impact actually threw me several inches up off the floor. The air filled with smoke. It all happened so fast—there was no time to even be afraid. As soon as it was over, we made our way outside so we wouldn't suffocate from all the gunpowder smoke.

The first thing I noticed was the debris all around our gun. Shrapnel had ripped the gun full of holes. The barrel of this huge gun pointed about minus five degrees—a clear sign of serious damage. Normally, it was impossible for it to go below zero degrees. Later on, we discovered two bombs had fallen on top of the heap of soil that was there to protect us and the ammunition. Those bombs had fallen only four or five metres from where we were lying on the floor. An even greater miracle was that one of the bombs had landed right on top of the four inches of concrete which covered the ammunition! That one hadn't exploded, even though it had landed on some of the most sensitive ammunition we ever used! As we exited the bunker, I became fully aware of the danger that surrounded us.

A few days later, enemy planes started dropping bombs all around us again. We all jumped into a nearby trench. As I lay less than half a metre below ground level, bombs exploded and shrapnel flew in all directions. Suddenly, I heard a buzzing sound like a propeller. Shrapnel shot into the ground about twenty-five centimetres from my head! Later, I poked into this hole and tried to dig out the shrapnel with my jackknife, but I couldn't find it. Praise God, it hadn't hit me!

Since I had left home a few months ago, I hadn't found a friend, relative, or anyone from our Mennonite people with whom I felt close. Then one day, when about a hundred or more teenagers had gathered together in a large room, the officer in charge asked each of us to rise and identify ourselves. To my surprise, one rose to his feet and identified himself as Peter Friesen—a Mennonite! I didn't waste any time making his acquaintance. I discovered he had come from my neighbouring village in Russia. For a time we kept in touch, but as it was war, we lost contact. But it was good to have someone to share with, even if just for a short time.

As the Americans came closer and closer, and we had run out of ammunition to bring down their planes, those in charge decided to release us from military duty. Before fully dismissing us, however, the officer made an announcement asking for volunteers to bring down American tanks. Out of our group of fifty or more, only one idiot made himself available for this craziness.

They assigned the rest of us to one of the older soldiers, a low-ranking officer, to lead us from place to place to hide from the enemy. The first night they gave us a place to stay in an underground bunker. To make

This photo of my friend Peter Friesen (on the left) and I was taken at the Immigration Camp in Gronau, Germany, 1947.

room for us to sleep at night, we first had to empty it of unexploded bombs. We carefully took them out and deposited them into a nearby ditch.

We continued to be led from place to place. It was about this time that I lost my friend Peter Friesen. As a result, I felt alone again. They took us to some large military armouries, two or three stories high. We stayed in the lower floor, which was almost like a basement. One day some of these foolish teenage recruits found some balloons, filled them with gas, tied a string to them, and let them float up into the air. The Americans, being close by, took note of them and must have surmised that they came from a German military installation. They promptly answered with artillery, firing one shot after another into our building. Glass and other debris fell as the grenades crashed in. It was scary!

But thus far, God had kept me safe.

Another time one of the German officers asked me to help him carry some bicycle parts to a place for repair. As he walked ahead of me, I noticed he kept his head bent down, yet often looked behind himself, as if someone were on his heels and about to hit him on the head. I knew what this meant, so I followed his example. Sure enough, a few minutes later the Americans fired shots at us. We hadn't seen them, but they had obviously seen us. When the first grenade landed nearby, the officer jumped into a hole big enough for only one person to duck his head below ground level. There wasn't a second one for me to hide in! I noticed a steel fence close by with a concrete foundation about thirty centimetres high. I flopped down behind it. Unfortunately, the American artillery came from the side where I was lying. It was impossible to jump over this steel fence to lie down on the other side for more protection. I had no choice, though; I had to do what could be done.

They hit a building a stone's throw away. It ignited at once and started to burn. I was lying there, listening to shrapnel flying in all directions. At one point, I knew it was too risky for me to stay put any longer. I knew I was risking my life by disobeying a military order, but I also knew one of these grenades could end my life at any moment. Since it was unmistakably clear that the American Army would soon overtake us, I decided to roll down to lower ground. I hid behind a few shrubs, then made my way down to the basement where the rest of our boys were. When I came in, some of the fellows stared at me as if to say, "What's with you?" I suppose I still looked petrified.

We continued to move from place to place. Since Peter Friesen had left, I connected with another fellow, named Roshik. He was from Poland, but of German descent.

One day I decided not to follow orders to keep moving. I didn't want to be a target for the Americans. At least we had some protection in this dark basement. I told Roshik about my intention and asked him if he would also defy orders. He agreed. I informed one of the older soldiers from a different division of my plan; he, too, supported my idea.

As expected, early in the morning of April 18, 1945, while still dark, our officer ordered all of us to line up outside to go somewhere else. I approached him and asked if it would be okay for me to stay where we were, because I really didn't think it helpful to keep moving. To my surprise, he said, *"Antreten muessen Sie, was Sie spaeter machen, ist Ihre Sache."* ("You have to line up. Whatever you do from then on is for you to decide.") My mind was made up; I lined up with the rest of them. When the moment arrived to start another march, I turned to my friend and said, "Let's go back into the basement." However, he became fearful and went with them anyway. Later on, one of these fellows told me that the Americans fired ferociously at them as they escaped.

Except for a few candles, it was dark in the basement. As I went in, I had to pass some of the older soldiers. One of them asked me why I had remained behind, as our group had left only minutes before. Acting ignorant, I asked, "Did they?"

Then the other soldier, with whom I had shared my plan, interrupted. "Come with me. I'll show you how to find your group." When we had walked out of earshot, he said, "Go outside to the other end of the building. You'll find another door. Go in there."

That's what I did. We sat in almost total darkness for a day or two, not even knowing what time of day it was. After some time, one of the soldiers burst in and announced that the American Army had conquered this part of Germany. He also told us it was eleven o'clock, just before noon. We went from almost total darkness outside into bright sunshine. Finally, for us the war had come to an end.

CHAPTER 12

The War Ends, POW Camp Begins

My new friend Roshik and I went to see a German family. I'm not sure why we went there. However, they advised us to go to the other side of the nearby river. We needed to cross a bridge so badly shattered by bombs that vehicle traffic could no longer use it. However, pedestrians could.

This family informed us of organized German groups called *Wehrwolf*. Their function was to work behind the scenes and stab the occupying army in the back. They offered us civilian clothing in exchange for our uniform, which we accepted. However, when they talked about joining another fighting organization, I thought to myself, *What are these people thinking? Do they think we're stupid?* I was so happy to see the fighting end, so I didn't reply to their suggestion.

As we left their home, I received another surprise. Roshik was actually going to take their advice and join the *Wehrwolf* gang! I said, "Are you out of your mind? We're finally free. It would be nothing short of suicide!" It didn't take long to persuade him to agree with my plan.

I had dreamed for many years of going to America. Three of my mother's sisters had immigrated to either the United States or Canada. From correspondence with them in the early 1930s, I had the impression that it was a good place to live. I also had high regard for Americans as a whole.

I wasn't afraid to fall into the hands of the Americans or the British. However, I *was* afraid to fall into the hands of the Russians. I wanted no part of them. The presence of the Americans gave me hope of someday going to America.

As we debated what to do, I remembered hearing rumours that if you had been in the German Army and hadn't reported to the American authorities, they would kill you. As we were inexperienced and had no idea what awaited us, we decided to look up someone from the American Army and report to them.

We walked to the city of Halle. Before long, we found two American soldiers on a street corner. I spoke to one of them, as I wasn't afraid and believed we would be treated fairly. He asked what we wanted. I told him we had been German soldiers. They asked me several times how old I was. I told them I was seventeen. I couldn't speak a word of English, and he wasn't much better in German, so I showed him by counting on my fingers. The moment I said "seventeen," he shook his head and said, "No, twelve!"

He led us behind the building where they had gathered another twenty-five to thirty German prisoners. First they ordered us to empty our pockets and backpack. They took anything that could possibly be used to harm anyone. I had a nice jackknife, which my father had given me; I could understand why they took that. However, they also took my small mirror and comb. Fortunately, they let me keep all my clothing, a blanket, and my backpack. From some of the older soldiers, they even took a bag full of sugar and threw it on a manure pile.

From here, they took us to a large farm and dropped us off next to another manure pile. They checked all our belongings again and took anything that suited them. Many prisoners ended up without an overcoat or a blanket. The day I became a prisoner of war was sunny and warm. It also happened to be Adolf Hitler's birthday—April 20, 1945!

From there, they took us in army trucks to Eisleben. The prison camp was located outdoors behind barbed-wire fences next to a mountain of slate. It was divided into sections separated by more barbed wire. Thousands of prisoners filled each section.

After one or two sunny days, it turned cold again and started to rain. We had no tent, no shed, or anywhere else to take cover from the rain and chill. Thousands of us walked or milled around, trying to keep warm. Our clothing became soaking wet; we had no place to dry ourselves. The only thing we could do was take off our clothes, squeeze out as much water as possible, and put them back on again.

Our sleeping accommodations? Nothing but ankle-deep mud! We did have empty tin cans, which we used to push the mud aside to have a dry place to lie down for the night. However, it often rained day and night, making it impossible to sleep. We had to walk around all night trying to keep warm, which didn't really work. My feet were so cold; they felt like ice.

For the first two or three days, we were given fine food, the same as was given to the American soldiers.

These packs included a small can of meat, crackers, a chocolate bar, and four cigarettes. From then on, our daily ration became one loaf of white bread per three people. Soon that changed—one loaf for a hundred of us! For a long time, they gave us such things as a spoonful of sugar or flour, coffee, powdered milk, dried carrots or beets. These rations were so small, however, that it wouldn't have been enough to feed a cat. Worst of all, they treated us like cattle—we spent day and night in the mud, wet, and cold.

One day, they gave us one raw potato to eat. Another prisoner made a little fire and allowed me to put my potato in the hot ashes. When the fire died down, I rubbed off the ashes, put a little salt on it and ate it. I had never in my life eaten anything that tasted so good! I promised myself that if I were ever released from prison, that's the way I would eat *my* potatoes. How things have changed.

Since we received little to no food, we only needed to go to the bathroom once a week. That caused us enormous problems. Besides, our "bathroom" was a half-metre deep trench.

We spent about ten days in Eisleben. I'll never forget the first day of May. We not only had rain, but snow. Some of the prisoners sang in mockery, *"Der Mai ist gekommen, die Baueme schlagen aus."* ("May has arrived, the trees are budding.") However, not a tree or flower was in sight.

At the beginning of May, they loaded us like cattle into American trucks—squashed together with standing room only. As the truck filled, some of the American soldiers stepped up and pushed with all their might against the ones at the back, murmured something in English, then pushed again. We were so close to one another that if someone had fainted or collapsed, he wouldn't have been able to sit or lie down.

It was a lengthy trip from Eisleben (near Leipzig,) to Sinzig (near Andernach), just north of Koblenz. It was approximately three hundred kilometres, as the crow flies, but at least four hundred kilometres by road. We stood for endless hours.

On one of the stops along the way, the driver ordered everyone to hand over their valuables, such as watches and jewellery. They threatened to shoot anyone who wouldn't obey this order. We finally arrived in Sinzig, on the Rhine River. This camp was much larger than the one in Eisleben. They imprisoned three hundred thousand POWs at this site, under the same conditions as Eisleben! It was so large, you couldn't see from one end of the camp to the other.

This camp, too, was divided into sections with barbed wire, with thousands of people in each section. This part of Germany received a lot of rain. The beginning of May was not only wet, but also mighty cold. We were soaking wet, had no dry clothes to change into, and no means to dry our wet clothing. We could only hope the sun would come out to dry them.

It eventually did get a bit warmer, but the rain wouldn't stop. Once, while it was still exceedingly cold, four of us took empty tin cans and dug a hole to lie down in at night. I was the only one who possessed a military blanket; the other three had nothing but the clothes on their backs. We made the hole just big enough for the four of us to lie down side by side. We used my blanket to stretch across the hole and fastened it with whatever splinter of wood we could find to keep the cold wind out.

After we were tucked in for the night, but before any of us had fallen asleep, it began to rain again. As you can imagine, the blanket was soon soaked. A stream of water poured down into the middle of our "bedroom!" Now what? Well, we each took an empty gallon-sized tin can and sat down on it, one in each corner. This was only a temporary solution, however, because water continued to pour down from the sky. The water began to rise in the hole until we couldn't stay any longer. We had to go back to the old way and again get soaking wet.

When daylight finally arrived, the campsite looked more like a lake than a pasture! It continued to rain day after day; there seemed to be no end in sight. Finally, it did stop. We dried our clothing, partly by the sun and partly from body heat.

On another occasion, perhaps in July, I woke up in the middle of the night with a strange feeling. Still drowsy, I groped around me with my hand and realized I was lying in water several inches deep! I was soaking wet again, but at least it wasn't so cold.

My biggest fear was dying of starvation. Many times, when I tried to get up from a sitting position or from lying on the ground, I felt dizzy. I saw black in front of my eyes. I had to sit or lie down, then try it again. After five or six attempts, I was finally able to get up and walk around.

As difficult as it was, someone always found ways to make it even more miserable. Because everyone was hungry, some would cheat and steal food from others. However, anyone caught in the act would sorely regret his action later. Many times at early dawn, I heard some-one receiving a merciless strapping and begging for mercy. As soon as the first screams of pain pierced the air, I heard voices from all around shouting, *"Hout ihn! Hout ihn!"* ("Hit him! Hit him!")

Then they cut a strip out of his hair from front to back and another from one side to the other. Next, they made him stand on top of a forty-gallon steel drum, with a large sign around his neck. It said, *"Ich bin ein Dieb"* or *"Ich habe meine Kameraden bestohlen."* ("I'm a thief" or "I've stolen from my comrades.") I recall seeing them on this drum for hours. Sometimes they had to stand on top of it all day.

Towards the end of my time in the camp, the Americans ordered a large group of us to line up and get ready for a march from Sinzig to Andernach. This would have been about twenty-five kilometres, as the crow flies, but several kilometres longer by road. As nearly starved individuals, you can imagine how difficult it was to take a walk like this. After walking for some distance, we stopped for a rest. Here some German people served us food; how we appreciated that! When we finally arrived in Andernach, the situation remained the same—thousands of prisoners behind barbed wire. It's a good thing it was warm in July and August.

In the meantime, the Allies had divided Germany into four sections: the American, British, French, and Russian zones. The French military controlled the part where we stayed. We clearly noticed the change by the way they fed us. The Americans gave us the finest food, albeit very little; it was truly a starvation diet. We received somewhat more in the French camp, but it looked like swine food. Their tasteless potato soup looked almost like the mud we lay in.

Besides the poor food, I witnessed an act of brutality one day only a stone's throw away. When we heard a banging noise, we looked up and saw French soldiers whacking defenseless German prisoners over the head with the shaft of a rifle. If they attempted to get up, they would receive another blow, until they couldn't rise again. I was shocked! I had never seen anything like this. Someone told me those killed in this fashion were from the "SS" (*Schutzstaffel*, or Defense Squadron). It was hard to comprehend how a person could be so heartless and kill a defenseless human being in such merciless fashion.

Things did become a bit better. While the French never gave us any delicacies, toward the end we received enough potatoes to fill our empty stomachs. Sometimes the German people came to the fence and handed out small packages of food. However, with such a multitude, few received even a morsel. I was one of the unfortunate, but I did survive.

One day, either in Sinzig or Andernach, I met my friend Peter Friesen again amongst the thousands of prisoners! We had been separated for a long time. From then on, we never lost contact again, even to this very day.

I spent nearly four months in this prison, from April 20 to August 8, 1945. Others stayed even longer. Many didn't survive, as the conditions were so severe. According to reports, dead bodies were carried out of the camp every day.

Many years later, in the 1950s, I finally made contact with my parents and siblings. They told me again and again how they had prayed for me. While I was not spared from difficult times, I believe their prayers kept me alive and always hopeful.

Decades later, people asked, "Weren't you afraid you would die in those conditions? Didn't you ferociously hate the Allies for what they did to you? Weren't you terribly angry, depressed, or hopeless?" I know many who had those feelings; personally, I didn't. I'm sure it was because I had a godly family praying for me. It never even occurred to me that I would die there. My explanation for those most miserable conditions was simply this: "It was wartime, and it was tough."

I was also not aware that these conditions were created deliberately. I found out much later that this could have been avoided. In fact, decades later I read in American magazines that Eisenhower had wanted to starve all those German prisoners to death. He made it a crime punishable by death for German civilians to feed prisoners! Even knowing that, I have never allowed anger or revenge to take hold of me. Sometimes it's better not to know everything.

CHAPTER 13

Freedom at the Drehers

Our imprisonment finally ended. First, they released the clergy—after them, those under eighteen. Peter and I were in this category, even though he had turned eighteen only two months earlier. On August 8, 1945, we received official word of our freedom. We left the camp the next day. As long as I live, I will never forget two birthdays—Adolph Hitler's on April 20, the day I became a prisoner of war, and my birthday on August 8, the day I was finally set free!

Once more, the question came to our minds, "What now?" We didn't know a soul in all of Germany. All I knew was that I wanted to be as far away from Communism as possible. First, we went to a railroad station. Here they gave us nourishing, traditional German *Erbsensuppe,* a type of pea soup, free of charge. They also gave a free train ride to anyone just released from a prison camp. Of course, we didn't have a dime to our name at the time.

We took a train going west. Eventually, we needed to change trains. As we were waiting for our next one to arrive, Peter left me for a little while to get some information. When he returned, I was still waiting. He told me that someone had informed him of the whereabouts of his family; they had been sent back to Russia. He wanted to leave me and reunite with his family. I was stunned, to say the least. I tried my utmost to persuade him not to even *consider* such a thing.

I remember clearly asking him, "What can you possibly do for your family by going back to Communist Russia? We've come from this tyrannical system and you want to go back voluntarily and suffer, now that you're free?"

I will never forget his reply: *"Wan de daut uthole kene, dann kaun eck daut uk."* ("If they can take it, so can I.")

For me, there was nothing in the world that could have persuaded me to go back to live as a slave under Joseph Stalin! I was fed up with that system; I couldn't imagine anything worse.

Peter said goodbye and left me. Now I was alone again, but I wasn't worried. My goal remained to live in the free world; I wanted to go to America someday. Suddenly, while I was still waiting for my train, Peter returned. To my delight, he had changed his mind after all!

When our train arrived, we continued our journey west to a place called Langenlonsheim. As we sat in the waiting room, two German girls came to talk to us. They asked us where we were from and where we wanted to go. We only knew we wanted to be as far away from Communism as possible. When we told them this, and because we didn't know a soul in all of Germany, they asked if we would like to come with them. They both lived on farms not far from there.

We accepted their gracious offer and went along with them. These young ladies, about twenty years of age, were from different families in neighbouring villages. I ended up going with Elfriede Dreher. Her parents were Christoph and Frieda Dreher from the village of Kuelz, not far from Koblenz. Peter went to live in the nearby village of Neuerkirch with the Petrie family.

I found a good home at the Drehers, who were well-to-do farmers. One of the first things they did was check my weight on a scale. I weighed only ninety pounds! My normal weight should have been around 140 pounds.

The Drehers owned a number of horses, a dozen cows, some pigs, and chickens. Every morning they gave me as much heated milk as I wanted. They had enough bread and potatoes to eat. Although they had a large farm, they were required to sell a fair portion of their goods to the community; after all, it was just after the war. Items such as butter and meat were a rarity. For breakfast, we ate bread spread with cottage cheese mixed with milk and a little salt. I actually found that quite tasty.

Each household took turns baking wonderful German bread in the community bakehouse. I helped on the farm and in the barn. The Drehers never forced me to do more than I could. They were good-hearted and intelligent people.

Mr. Dreher had been the mayor of the village and his wife was a leader in a women's organization in the community. As a rule, they didn't attend church. However, they never kept me from doing so. The neighbouring village, where Peter lived, had an Evangelical Lutheran church, which I attended regularly. Later we attended the *Evangelische Freie Gemeinde,* which was much like a Baptist church, in a small city named Simmern about five kilometres from where I lived. When the Dreher sons found out Peter and I went to such a group, they sneered.

Before long, Peter and I became acquainted with Rev. Isaak Loewen, his wife, and his son Victor. They were immigrants from the Odessa area in Russia.

I needed to learn a new language while staying with the Drehers, or at least a different dialect. While they spoke German, sometimes I couldn't understand what they were saying. Once their daughter Elfriede told me, *"Jakob, ge mal in de schauer an hul a mal a man."* I didn't have a clue what she was saying. In German, we would say, *"Jakob, geh mal in die Scheune und hole mir einen Korb."* ("Jacob, go to the barn and fetch me a basket.") Before long, we learned to communicate. I have never found it difficult to learn a new language or dialect.

Other friends and villagers in the surrounding area soon knew that the Drehers had added a new member to their family. One day, one of their friends spoke to me when he arrived at the farm for a visit. While visiting inside with the Drehers, he asked them, "Where's this boy you told me about, the one born in Russia and just released from the prisoner of war camp?"

"You just spoke to him," they told him.

He responded, *"Dea schwaetzt ja gnau so wie die unseren!"* ("He speaks just like we do!")

Apparently, I had learned their dialect rather quickly.

Decades later, when my wife and I visited the Drehers, we recalled some of those humorous experiences. I told them that I had understood little of what Elfriede had said. However, I had heard something about "a man," so I concluded she probably wanted me to get her a man. Then I asked myself, *But isn't that something she should do on her own?* After sharing this, they almost laughed their heads off!

I remember numerous other humorous anecdotes. Elfriede's twenty-three-year-old brother Otto found humour in almost any situation. One day he went to his friend's wedding in the village. The young bride had become pregnant before the wedding; therefore, they wouldn't allow her to wear a white dress. Since the rest of his family had not been invited, he shared every detail of it when he returned. He said that the new bride had worn a dark dress instead of white. Otto's mother asked curiously in their *Hunsruecker Platt* dialect, *"Was hat dan der Para gsat?"* ("What did the minister have to say about that?") Like out of a pistol, Otto responded, *"Dea para hot gsot, Huchzeit, hohe Zeit, und fuer Euch zwei ist es hoegste Zeit!"* It doesn't translate well into English, but the gist of it is, "It's high time for the two of you to get married!"

One day, the Drehers purchased a horse—a cause for celebration! Most farmers in the area worked their fields with either oxen or cows, but the Drehers had a number of horses. By the time the men came home with this new animal, it was evening and quite dark. Since there was no way to transport it in a trailer, they had to walk it all the way from a neighbouring village to their home.

After the men took the horse into the barn, they came into the house. That's when the excitement started. They discussed the deal backward and forward. Both the women and men asked questions: "How much did you pay for it?" "How old is it?" "How tall is it?" "What race is this horse?" "What color is it?" This went on for quite some time.

Finally, when everyone had received satisfactory answers to their questions, the seventy-one-year-old grandmother asked, *"Ist es denn auch ein brafer Gaul?"* ("Is it also a well-behaved horse?")

Otto replied, *"Grossmutter, es ist so ein braver Gaul, der hat den ganzen Weg von Kiesselbach bis daheim in den Stall, nicht eh Wort gschwaezt!"* ("Grandma, it's such a well-behaved horse, it didn't say a word all the way from Kiesselbach to our barn!")

Otto, at the age of twenty-three, became engaged to a lovely young lady from a neighbouring village. They made plans and prepared for the big day as the wedding came closer. One day they asked me to be the *Kellner*, the one who would serve wine at the tables. I told them I had never developed a taste for wine or any other alcoholic beverages. I agreed to serve it, but assured them I didn't care for it myself. They didn't believe me and teased me about getting drunk at the wedding. It was all said in good humour.

This was the first wedding I attended in my entire life. The family invited a minister to perform the cere- mony at their residence. I sensed a good spirit between the minister and the Dreher family. I did serve the wine, taking a sip here and there, but I didn't become drunk, as they wanted me to. It turned out to be a good day.

CHAPTER 14

My Apprenticeship with Mr. Lang

After being with the Drehers for a little more than a year, I started looking for a place to learn cabinet-making. After all, I had learned some woodworking from my father. One day I met a fine young Christian man in the village who owned a shop with all the necessary power tools. However, he wasn't permitted to have an apprentice, since he didn't have his Master's degree in the trade.

A short time later, someone informed me about a small cabinet-making factory owned by Christoph Lang, in the village of Rigenroth, about ten kilometres from where I lived. I was warned, however, that Mr. Lang wouldn't be the easiest person to work for, especially as an apprentice. However, no one knew of a better place.

I went to meet Mr. Lang. He asked me many questions about where I was from and what I knew about the trade. I got the impression that it was important to him to know as much as possible about my skill in woodworking. He had a fourteen-year-old apprentice, but he needed one more. I was nineteen at the time.

He expected me to sign up for a three-year apprenticeship. I told him I had been corresponding with relatives in America and intended to emigrate there. I didn't want to commit myself to him for three years and not be able to pursue that dream. At first, he hesitated. He said once I had signed the contract, I would be expected to stay to the end of the term.

I asked him if he would be willing to hire me simply as an employee. He wasn't willing to do that. I made it clear I wouldn't sign a contract unless he agreed to permit me to terminate the apprenticeship the moment I had an opportunity to emigrate. Finally, he agreed; I signed the document.

I began a new life. We agreed that I would stay on the premises and receive room and board. My wages for the first year were 50 D.M. (Deutsche Mark) per month. Since he provided room and board, he kept 46 D.M., which left me with only 4 D.M. Of course, this was next to nothing; one American cigarette cost 4 D.M. on the black market.

Immediately after the war, you couldn't buy anything anyway, unless you found it on the black market.

To get to my bedroom, I had to go through a breeze-way, up an open stairway, and through a wood storage room. The bedroom had three beds and a window, a third of which was covered with plywood. It had an old wall unit for clothing. Four or five of us would live here (including one other apprentice and a number of Lang's employees). There were three beds for the five of us. The room looked unkempt and dirty.

The apprentices had to rise early to do the chores before the regular employees started their day. There were only two of us at the beginning, and we took turns starting the fire and taking care of the cattle in the barn; it was considered normal for an apprentice to spend most of his time in the barn and field the first year. However, since I was nineteen and had considerable knowledge in wood-working, Mr. Lang allowed me to be in the shop most of the time. Because I was over eighteen, he also allowed me to operate his power tools. The other apprentice, Theodor, who was only fourteen, didn't have that privilege, even though he had started working before me.

The work itself wasn't bad; the difficult part was having Mr. Lang for a master. Everyone feared him; nothing was good enough for him. No matter how hard we tried, he would find something to scream about. When he became angry, he turned all red in the face. His wife and children feared him, too. When the time came for me to leave, his seventeen-year-old son Heinz said to me, "I wish I were in your shoes." He wanted no part of being with his father. No one could stand him.

On my first day, I was assigned to carry some boards from one place to another and stand them up against the wall. My father had already taught me not to put boards against the wall at a 45-degree angle. I thought I had done a good job. However, when a senior employee came to inspect my work, he scolded me harshly for not even knowing how to stand up a board. He then demonstrated by putting one of them almost vertical to the wall.

I soon realized that the criticism, screaming, and putdowns were not to point out mistakes, but rather to say, "You're a nobody." I once heard a quote from one of the employees: *Was ist ein Lehrling? Ein Lehrling ist ein Individium das von den Gesellen geschlagen und getreten wird.* ("What is an apprentice? An apprentice is an individual to be beaten and kicked around by the employees.")

I had few problems with the senior foreman or any of the employees. They soon realized I was no novice when working with wood or tools. I even made friends with some of them. One of the best employees was the foreman—an excellent woodworker. He was a young married man with a small child. He once invited me to visit his home. After I left Mr. Lang's employ, we corresponded with one another.

Mr. Lang was a different story. Fortunately, he did a lot of traveling on business trips. It was always a great relief when he was gone.

Things were different here than what I had become used to at the Drehers. They served the meals for Theodor and me in a separate room with a couple of other employees. Only one of the employees had the privilege of eating with the Lang family in the dining room. The food was far from appetizing. We were given leftover crusts of bread for breakfast. Instead of butter or jam, we had to make do with *Eierschmier* (egg smear), a mixture of flour, water, and food colouring. It looked like pancake batter—highly unappetizing and fit for pigs. Lunch and dinner weren't much better.

Mr. Lang owned an old-model car—an Opel. However, no gasoline was available after the war. To make it drivable, they rebuilt it to use wood as fuel. They removed the trunk lid and placed what looked like a large water heater in the trunk. This unit functioned like a stove. Smoldering blocks of wood fuelled the unit. It had to be a special kind of hardwood, such as beech.

The fumes from the burning wood acted as a substitute for gasoline.

When Mr. Lang was ready to go on a trip, we filled the heater with wood blocks and lit a fire underneath. He could put several bags of wood blocks into this unit. He also had a box on the roof of the car where he put as many as eight bags full of wood. It was our job to chop the wood into approximately two-by-two-inch blocks. Anytime he wanted to go away, he called us to chop wood. It could be as early as two in the morning or late at night.

While I had the privilege of being in the shop most of the time, there were many exceptions to this rule. Mr. Lang often asked me to do jobs on the farm. He had a septic tank where the fluids from the manure pile accumulated. They pumped this out and took it to the fields to serve as fertilizer.

On one occasion, Mr. Lang and I worked together on this job. He first tried to do this with his own hand pump. After he found out it wouldn't work, he borrowed one from the neighbour. It had to be primed first by pouring water into it, but the water had to be carried from a pool about fifty metres away. He was a strong man, less than fifty years old; I was half his size and had been released from a prisoner of war camp a little more than a year earlier. I hurried with a pail of water in each hand to where he stood by the pump. He poured it in while I pumped the large handle up and down.

When he realized this pump was no better than his own, he shouted at the top of his voice, *"Pump doch mal!"* ("For goodness sake, start pumping!") When that didn't work, he ordered *me* to pour the water into the top of the pump. The hole was roughly one and a half metres off the ground with a ten-centimetre opening. I was only 5′ 6″, so I had to lift the pail full of water over my head and pour it into this small hole. Of course, some of it was spilled on the ground, whether he or I was the one pouring it in. He shouted again of the top of his voice: *"Giess doch nicht die Haelfte daneben!"* ("Don't dump half of the water on the ground!")

After numerous attempts, he became infuriated, raised the pump handle as high as possible, and slammed it down with all his might. Then he shouted, *"Der Deiwel soll die Pulpump hole!"* ("May the Devil come and get this pump!") I realized he was not interested in this piece of junk, either.

One day, after this septic tank had been emptied, Theodor and I had to climb down inside the stinky hole and clean it. We only had a broom and brush to clean the walls and floor. When we finished that job, we didn't dare go close to another human being; the "fragrance" from the manure stayed on our clothing for a long time. You might ask, "Why didn't you take a shower and change your clothing?" Well, there was no shower, and we had nothing to change into. When I put on a "clean shirt" washed by Mrs. Lang and went to visit the Dreher family, Mrs. Dreher looked at it and asked me if she could rewash it.

We had no money for buying new clothing, even if there had been some available. To purchase a new pair of pants or a work shirt, we needed to have connections and money. One day, Heinz, Mr. Lang's seventeen-year-old son, came into the shop wearing a new pair of workpants. The following night, while lying on our beds, someone in our room commented about the "master's son" having a new pair of pants, but none of us could buy anything.

Fourteen-year-old Theodor remarked how badly he needed a new pair of pants.

Paul, one of the senior employees, said, "Theo, you need a lot more than new pants."

Theo, with pity in his voice and tears in his eyes, asked, "What else do you think I need?"

"Sometimes you need a flat hand in your face," Paul said.

That ended the conversation. Yes, every now and then we had a good laugh.

Another unforgettable situation took place on the lower level of the shop where they had a kiln to dry lumber. A boiler in a hole provided the power to run it. The mechanism had an electric motor with a belt on a pulley. This contraption somehow controlled the steam. Since everything was old and worn out, the belt kept falling off. Whenever that happened, moments later there would be a loud, almost explosive puff of steam exiting the system, just like an old steam locomotive.

Theodor and I had to look after this outdated and useless piece of machinery. Sometimes we spent a couple of hours playing around with it to keep the belt on the pulley, even before we ate breakfast. One day it was my turn to look after the boiler. It must have been around ten o'clock in the morning when I finally had it working and went to eat breakfast.

Mr. Lang was in the process of remodelling his house, so the garage, with all the clutter and junk, became our "dining room." I had barely started to eat when Mr. Lang came storming in. I could hear him shouting before I even saw him. He stopped about a metre in front of me, erect as a pole, head bent backwards, hands flailing, and shouted at the top of his voice, *"Natuerlich, Herr General am Kaffeetisch!"* ("Of course, the Lord General at the dining table!") Following this outburst, he continued to call me a stupid idiot to be sitting there feeding my face while all hell had broken loose at the boiler.

I knew immediately what I had to do. He stormed on ahead of me as we went to the lower level. I jumped down and put the belt back on the pulley. All of a sudden, a burst of steam shot out! While we were used to this frightening sound, Mr. Lang was not. The sound scared him so badly that he looked like he had been electrocuted. When he realized what a fool he had made of himself, he grabbed a steel rod from behind him, lifted it up as if to strike me, and shouted, *"Ich schlag dich tot!"* ("I'll kill you!")

In the early morning before the other employees began to work, Theodor and I took the ashes out of the fireboxes of the heating system and lit the fire. One day Mr. Lang came looking for me in the heating area and showed me an item way back in the heating unit that didn't belong there. He shouted that I was the biggest idiot he had ever come across. He hit me across the head with his powerful right hand. I nearly fell over. He smacked me again with his left hand. Then he complained that his hand hurt. He said, *"Meine Hand ist mir zu schade."* ("I feel sorry for my hand.")

The foreman, who witnessed this, became furious with how the boss had treated me. He said, "If something like this ever happens again, come and see me. I'll look after it." Fortunately, it never happened again. However, it caused some hearing loss. I'm not sure if I ever totally recovered from it, at least not if you ask my wife.

I corresponded with my relatives in America from time to time. One day, Mr. Lang had the nerve to open my mail from a relative in Canada. Since I didn't have an address or a mailbox of my own, it came to me in care of his address. He called me to his office and read part of my letter to me. He found out that my request to emigrate was in progress.

"Hey, you, what's going on here?" he asked. "You haven't even been with me a full year. What's with you? What are you thinking?"

When I reminded him of our earlier agreement, he scorned me. *"Ja, du fahr mal nach Amerika, dort werden dir die gebratenen Tauben ins Maul fliegen, da brauchst nur das Maul aufsperren!"* ("You go to America. There the roasted pigeons will fly right into your mouth. All you need to do is open your mouth wide!")

I went to the Drehers from time to time to visit. Since there was no public transportation, I walked the ten kilometres. On one occasion, I had understood that I was invited to stay for the night. However, toward the end of the day, I discovered that this was not the case. I got ready to leave as quickly as possible, but realized I wouldn't make it home before dark. I had to walk through at least two villages plus quite a stretch of dark forest. I didn't get far before darkness overcame me. I had no flashlight or lamp. Even though there were no lions or tigers in the area, I knew dogs or wild boars could attack me. As I walked along the muddy road, I heard sounds of creatures roaming around not too far away. I won't admit to being scared to death, but I was a bit uncomfortable at times.

One day I bartered with Heinz for an old bike he put together with parts from a number of other bicycles. I gave him some American cigarettes, which were much in demand after the war. This bike made it easier to go from place to place. Instead of taking the shortcut through the dark and muddy forest, I could stay on the gravel roads through several villages.

One night on my way home, it was almost pitch dark and completely silent. All of a sudden, a dog leaped at my feet and made ferocious sounds. I couldn't see him, but I could feel him at my feet. I kicked him, whereupon he became even more vicious. Finally, the owner called him off and I escaped unharmed.

On another night, I returned from visiting my friend Peter in Neuerkirch. As I entered the village of Kuelz, I heard someone about fifty metres behind me ask, "What time is it?" As this man approached, he opened a large jackknife; the blade reflected in the moonlight. I had no idea what this fellow might be up to.

A shock charged through me! I didn't attempt to get away from him, but he must have realized I was uneasy. He said he had passed through this village some time ago and a large dog had attacked him. The story ended well for both of us; there was no dog in sight that night.

While serving my apprenticeship, I stuck with my plan to immigrate to North America. I had no close friends in Germany and no knowledge of the whereabouts of my parents and family. I made plans to go and reside in an immigration camp in the British sector of Germany. I notified Mr. Lang of my intention and reminded him of the agreement I had signed with him. He wasn't at all pleased, but he finally got the message. He practically begged me to stay a little longer, so he could find another apprentice to replace me. It felt good when he made it clear I had been useful to him. He asked me to stay an extra two or three weeks. I agreed with his request, in return for a copy of my apprenticeship contract. He promised to do that, so I stayed.

The atmosphere of those last few weeks was negative and depressing. I thought the best thing would be to disappear secretly at night without attempting to bid him farewell. However, until the last day, he still hadn't given me a copy of my apprenticeship. This was important to me, because I wanted to have credit for the experience and time I had invested. I finally approached him, asked for it, and he gave it to me. That was the last time I went to bed at that place.

I had arranged with the milk deliveryman for a ride to the railway station in the nearest city. He always came early, so I had my few belongings packed and ready to go. Off I went to Gronau, in Westphalia, near the Dutch border.

I visited Mr. Lang and his wife in 1973. He pretended not to remember me, but I certainly had not forgotten him!

CHAPTER 15

Immigration Camp

Many Mennonite people from Russia had come to Gronau, Germany. After staying for one night with a friend's family, the immigration officials gave me a place to stay in the small neighbouring town of Epe. Here, as in Gronau, they accommodated us in large halls divided into smaller sections. They strung wires across the room and fastened blankets over them to create separate areas for each family. Each section had a blanket at the entrance to give people a little privacy.

As the "walls" were not soundproof, everyone could hear what you said, unless you whispered. All the beds were bunks. Anyone sleeping on the upper bunk could see across the entire hall, because the blanket walls were only as high as the top bunk. Since I was single, I had to share a section with another person. Of course, this was a temporary situation—a place for those waiting to go to Canada. The Canadian government first accepted immigrants who had close relatives there, providing they were in good health, especially their eyes and lungs.

Immigration camp was not a life of luxury; no one expected it to be. We received a daily ration of food—nothing too mouth-watering—but we didn't go to bed hungry. Unfortunately, most of the time we had little or nothing to do. Sometimes we listened to the stories of widows who had lost their husbands in the war, or who were still in Russia. These women often talked about the food. They would say things like, "The food wouldn't be so bad if only they'd put a little more fat in it." Old Mr. Thiessen once said, *"Jo, schen met bota derchjebrot, schmakjt irjedswaut got, an wan it en tobtoak es, oda ne ole colosch."* ("Nicely cooked with butter, anything tastes good—even a dishcloth or a pair of galoshes.")

I came to realize the disadvantage of not having anything to do. One day a truckload of coal arrived, and someone asked for volunteers to help unload it. My first thought was, *I don't want to do this.* Then I asked myself, *Why shouldn't I? I've worked all of my life; why not now?* Then I went to work without a second thought.

As we each waited anxiously for our turn to go to Canada, the process seemed to progress more quickly for some than others. I stayed in the immigration camp from October 12, 1947 to the beginning of June 1948. The wait seemed endless, especially when I saw others board the ship to the "Promised Land."

The reason most of us wanted to leave was because there was no future for us in Germany. The whole country was in ruins. Bombs had flattened the cities. One could only dream of finding a comfortable house to live in. There was nothing for sale. You couldn't even buy a shoestring or a nail. If you wanted to buy something in the town of Epe, you had to go through a trading centre. For example, if you owned a watch but needed a pair of socks or a shirt, you could have your watch displayed in a store window with a note saying what you wanted to trade it for.

During the wait, I became acquainted with several Mennonite Central Committee (MCC) workers from Canada and the United States. Siegfried Janzen directed the camp in Gronau. Others included Heinrich Janzen, C.F. Klassen, Rev. Johann Wichert, Arthur Voth, and Peter Dueck from the United States. I also started attending a Mennonite Brethren church in Gronau. The lead pastor was Jacob Peters, a loved and respected man who loved the Lord. Here I was baptized upon the confession of my faith and received as a member of the church.

From time to time, I went to see Siegfried Janzen to see if he had made any progress on my paperwork. He would say, "My office is expecting your papers to arrive soon." I noticed others in my category had left long ago, but I was still waiting. Every time I spoke to him, he gave me the same response.

One day I decided to try something on my own. I took a train to Hanover to see Mr. Arthur Voth, who directed a different camp for immigrants going to Canada. I met him in his office and told him of my concern. He was most gracious and caring and promised to look into my situation. I thanked him for his time and willingness to listen and went back to Gronau. Lo and behold, I soon received notice that Mr. Voth had located my papers in Heidelberg, in the American sector of Germany. From then on, things progressed rapidly.

I was told to go to Fallingbostel, between the cities of Soltau and Walsrode (north of Hanover and south of Hamburg.) This was the last gathering place before boarding a ship to Canada. The Mennonite Central Committee actually gave us the option of flying instead of sailing, but flying didn't sit well with any of us. They also gave us the opportunity to learn English. I immediately took advantage of that. However, after only a few lessons, they called me to get ready to board ship. My dream was about to come true; I was on the road to freedom!

To board the ship, we first went by train through the Netherlands, to Rotterdam. While there, I had the strange feeling I would see this part of the world again.

CHAPTER 16

Sailing to Canada

We boarded the *Volendam*, a large Dutch vessel that carried many Mennonite immigrants to both North and South America. Our journey began June 10, 1948, and ended in Quebec ten days later on June 20. When we left Rotterdam, it was smooth sailing, because we were still inland—fifty kilometres from the North Sea. However, as soon as we entered open water, our circumstances changed dramatically. I could distinctly see where the calm water ended and the restless North Sea began. Within seconds, the large ship began to rock.

We made a brief stopover in Southampton, England. After this, we sailed straightaway to Canada. Before this trip, I had never even been close to an ocean. Now I saw nothing but water and sky for the next ten days. Things

The Volendam, which brought me from Germany to Canada

went quite well; I didn't experience any seasickness the entire way across the open sea.

Siegfried Janzen sailed with us to give some guidance, information, and answers to our questions and concerns. One day he asked for volunteers to help serve in the dining room. The remuneration would be $2 per day. That wasn't bad in those days. Besides, I only had to work a few hours—during meals and shortly after them. I volunteered, but soon found myself in trouble. Since the dining room was located deep within the ship, rather than on the open deck, I came close to getting seasick; others weren't so fortunate. Whenever a fellow passenger vomited in the dining room, we servers had to clean it up. I couldn't handle that. I resigned and decided to make my money an easier way, once I arrived in Canada.

Our sleeping area was located deep down inside the ship, below sea level. We had no windows—just electric lights. Some of the passengers had a rough time with seasickness. I had little trouble, as long as I could stay on the open deck and see what was going on. Even being down in our sleeping quarters didn't bother me, as long as I was lying in bed. However, as soon as I sat up or walked around, I felt woozy.

Some of us decided to outwit seasickness. As soon as we got out of bed in the morning, we slipped on our pants, grabbed the rest of the clothing, and ran up to the open deck to finish dressing. It worked every time!

On days with severe storms and huge waves, I tried to find a seat as close as possible to the middle of the ship. I sat and watched the waves thrust the ship up and down. I noticed that when this enormous vessel dipped down, it seemed like the water almost flowed over the bow of the ship. When it came back up, it was way above the horizon.

One day we watched a smaller vessel rocking from side to side. It looked like it could tip over anytime. When our passengers noticed this, they all rushed to the side of the boat to observe this dangerous situation. As a result, our vessel began to tilt noticeably to that side!

One day they announced we were experiencing *Windstaerke acht* ("wind force eight," or tropical storm winds). On one of those days, I was standing on one of the decks above the water when a huge wave came crashing in. Immediately, tons of water filled the area. After this, they closed off the area with some heavy tarps.

As the days went by, we became more and more eager to see land. We finally arrived in Quebec City harbour. We stayed one more night on the ship, but the next day we were allowed to go ashore and look around. That day I took my first step onto Canadian soil. Actually, it was a giant leap on my long road to freedom!

I soon noticed some of our people walking around with something strange in their hand. At first, it looked like a carrot. However, I noticed the shape of the cone was far too steep, and it appeared to have a head on top. Then I saw them *licking* this thing. I moved closer and asked someone, "What is that?" He said, "Ice cream." He showed me a little store about a stone's throw away where I bought one for a mere five cents. I had heard about such a delicacy, but had never seen or tasted it. I have eaten it many, many times since.

CHAPTER 17

On the Farm in Port Rowan

Soon I was put on a train bound for my final destination. Since I could not speak English, someone pinned a label on my lapel indicating my name, the name of my relatives, and the ones who would meet me at my final destination.

Everyone headed off to different provinces. I left for Port Rowan, Ontario, near Simcoe. The train took me directly there, where I met my Uncle Jake Enns and Aunt Luise, my mother's oldest sister. They took me to their home only six miles from the station. Finally, I realized my dream of having arrived in the "New World." However, I hadn't come to Canada with the idea of living off my "rich relatives," as I heard some people comment. I was fully prepared to work and continue my apprenticeship as a cabinetmaker. That's why I had insisted my former boss, Mr. Lang, give me a copy of the contract.

Many things in Canada were different than in Germany. For example, Canadians had their own automobiles, which looked good in the photos they had sent to their relatives in Europe. I soon found out many of them were in poor condition. My uncle drove a 1941 Ford; it was one of the better ones in the community. Many still drove vehicles from the 1930s—even from the 1920s. I didn't see a major four-lane highway anywhere, which had been common in Germany. Yes, there was a paved road from Port Rowan to my uncle's place. However, when you arrived at a bridge, you had to stop and wait for the car approaching from the other direction; it was only wide enough for one vehicle at a time. I also noticed that neighbours lived far apart—not crowded together, as in Germany.

The schools were much different from the ones I attended in Russia. Our village, with a population of about two thousand, had two large schools. One of them was a large two-story building with at least fifteen teachers. In Port Rowan, they had a small, rural, one-room building for all seven or eight grades with only one teacher. I had never seen anything like it. It was right across the street from where I lived. I'm sure the ones in the cities must have been different.

My aunt and uncle lived on a paved road with a long dirt driveway; it wasn't even covered with gravel. In spring, or during the rainy season, it became so muddy that my uncle had to leave his car near the road for fear of getting stuck. They lived in a small house with no indoor plumbing. The water supply came from a well. They drew it up with a pail, as we did in Russia. They had no furnace—only an oil heater in one room. They had cabinets in the kitchen, but no sink or running water. Neither did they have a fridge or freezer—not even an icebox to keep dairy products and meat cold.

I'm getting water from the well.

They used a hole under the house as a storage place, whenever it wasn't flooded with water. I felt sorry for my Aunt Luise, a registered nurse who had become used to working at the Concordia Hospital in Winnipeg, with all its modern conveniences. When it did flood, it became my job to scoop up the water with a pail and throw it out the window; there was no pump.

To wash up for the weekend, the entrance to the house served as the washroom. You merely needed to close two doors and notify others of your need for privacy. They had no shower or tub; a large bowl with warm water was used to clean up. An outhouse was located not far from the house. They did have electricity in the house and barn, though.

Aunt Luise was a tidy woman and kept the house clean. She even had an old grand piano, which she played and sang along with. I had always wanted to play one. I tried a few times on my own, but soon realized I needed someone to teach me. I don't recall asking her to show me how, nor am I sure she could have done so.

My uncle's main work was in the barn. He had a 100-acre farm, but since he was past sixty, he rented his land to a neighbour. He had six milk cows; to make chores a bit easier, he purchased a milking machine. He also looked after some chickens and a few pigs. I helped him by taking the cows out to the pasture at the back of the farm in the morning and bringing them back in the evening.

Uncle Jake and Aunt Luise Enns' home.

Besides these chores, they had a small vegetable garden that needed to be weeded. It wasn't a full-time job and I didn't get paid for my work. However, they didn't charge me anything for room and board, and I didn't have to pay for anything else.

In August of 1948, I started working in the tobacco harvest. Even people who had their own grain farm worked in the tobacco fields, where they made good wages. My uncle and aunt also did this for about four to six weeks. I was grateful for the job, but was it ever hot! The soil was pure sand. In the morning, the plants were wet from dew, just like after a heavy rain. They were about six feet tall. There was enough room between the rows for a horse to pull what was called a "boat" — a long narrow box with runners like a sleigh.

*Here's how we planted tobacco. I'm the one on
the left side of the machine.*

My uncle drove the "boat" pulled by a horse. I was one of about six workers who removed the leaves from the bottom of each plant. They were almost at ground level, so we had to bend down all day. We kept at it until there was enough to fill the kiln. The rows seemed a mile long; there wasn't a chance to straighten up before the end of a row, either. I was the only one with no previous experience, so I had a hard time keeping up. The fellows who were used to it rushed to complete the job as soon as possible. Usually we finished shortly after lunch.

We had a particular method for doing this job. We picked with one hand. When that hand was full, we put the leaves under our other arm. When we couldn't hold any more, we emptied our armful into the "boat."

We started working at seven o'clock in the morning. We wore a raincoat, because the dew on the plants would soak our clothes otherwise. Around ten o'clock, the sun had dried up everything; then it became unbearably hot. Sometimes the temperature reached forty degrees Celsius in the shade. We couldn't walk barefoot in the sand without burning our feet.

It was an extremely dirty job. Our hands and clothing became covered with a layer of tar residue from the leaves, which was almost impossible to remove. We were given a special type of soap to clean our hands; it took some effort to remove that stuff. We threw away our clothing at the end of the season, since there was no way to clean them.

While the men picked leaves, the women tied them to sticks and put them on piles. After enough leaves were picked, the men hung them up in a kiln to dry. It took an hour or two to do this at the end of one day. We did this for several weeks. As time went by, we picked the leaves that grew higher on the stem of the plant; this meant less bending. Towards the end of the harvest, the leaves were waist high, which made it a lot easier. The first week was the most crippling. I noticed fellows my age in church on Sunday walking around with noticeably bent backs. Between the leaf-picking days, we pulled the suckers (wild shoots) from the plants—a less strenuous job.

We earned $10 per day—the same wages paid to General Motors workers. Grain farmers paid only $5 per day. Because of the hard work with good pay in the tobacco harvest, I repaid my trip to Canada quickly. Since my uncle had paid about $190 for my ticket, I only had to work nineteen days to repay it. That felt good! I believed what Scripture teaches: *"Owe nothing to anyone..."* (Romans 13:8). Someone once told me that a few immigrants still owed money for their boat tickets twenty-five years after coming to Canada!

The tobacco harvest was rather short, so I also worked in the fields on neighbouring farms. Farmers paid me up to sixty cents an hour. On one occasion, I was hired for a whole season. I received room and board, plus $25 per month. In the winter, I found work again with a tobacco farmer. We took the dried tobacco leaves from the sticks and sorted them. They paid me sixty cents an hour.

After I had paid for my trip, I did what I had decided to do long before coming to this country. I sent my friends back in Europe some of the goodies they had missed during and after the war—like cocoa, sugar, rice, and chocolate bars. It felt good to bless my friends with what I had craved so much during meagre times. I sent a parcel to my barber friend and a few items to the Drehers. However, I must confess, I didn't send anything to "Master Lang!"

After I had saved some money, I purchased an expensive wristwatch. It was a Savoy Incabloc, made in Switzerland; I paid $45 for it. That was a lot of money in those days, but it lasted twenty-five years. Later, in 1973, I bought a Bulova Accuquartz with a diamond on the face of it. I paid $325 for it; it also lasted twenty-five years.

I always loved music. I had learned to play a two-row button accordion in Germany. One day, in 1949, I went to Simcoe with my friends and bought one of these for $46. Before long, I joined a small orchestra composed of young people. From time to time, we presented a program in the church.

When I needed a haircut for the first time in my new country, I couldn't tell the barber how I wanted it done. My uncle had to come along and speak for me. I felt like a fool. Here I was—twenty years old—and I needed a sixty-year-old uncle to speak for me. I soon realized I would need three essential things: to learn English, to have my own vehicle, and to own a telephone.

I tried to pick up a few English words and phrases here and there, but it wasn't enough to carry on a conversation. I found out that there were free English classes in Simcoe forty kilometres from where I lived in Port Rowan. I didn't have my own vehicle, but three or four other young men were interested in taking some training classes at the same place. When I contacted them, they offered to take me along for a small fee.

My motorized bicycle

Before long, I was able to have simple conversations in English. As I moved from place to place, I continued studying the language. From 1952 to 1953, I took a year of Bible school. After that, I enrolled in a correspondence course to study English composition and mathematics from the American School in Chicago, which I found helpful. One day in 1950, while working in a basket factory in Grimsby, a lady asked me in perfect English, "Were you born in Canada?" That surprised me and encouraged me to learn even more.

My accordian, with my first car in the background.

In the spring of 1949, I decided to buy something with wheels. It was too soon to buy a car, and I also didn't have enough money for a decent motorcycle, but I heard about an ordinary bicycle with a small motor attached. I thought this would be better than pedaling ten kilometres to work, so I bought a used one. The problem, however, was that every now and then the spark plug would give me an electric shock on my knee. Occasionally, it even started my pants on fire!

My tall cousin Arnold Epp and I by my 1929 Model A Ford

Every now and then, I had mechanical problems with this contraption. I was neither trained to do mechanical repairs, nor did I have the tools. However, if the motor failed, I could pedal it like an ordinary bicycle.

By late 1949, I had saved enough money to buy an old car. My friend warned me, "When you have a car, it's like a bank; you put all your money into it, but you will never get it out." While this warning was appropriate, as I soon found out, I still couldn't get by without a car. I bought a 1929 Model-A Ford—a respectable vehicle for a twenty-year-old at that time.

Although it had a battery to start the engine, it also had a crank in front. If the battery failed, I could crank it. Of course, sometimes neither method worked, but there was still another way. I could ask two or three fellows to give me a push. I shifted into second or third gear, pushed the clutch in until I had the car moving about five miles per hour, then released it and, with good luck, away I went!

One day I went to Port Rowan, parked my car, and went about my business. When I was ready to leave, it wouldn't start. I tried to push it myself, then jump in, hoping it would start. After several failed tries, I saw two police officers heading my way. I had a beginner's license and could only drive legally if someone with a license sat beside me. I was sure I was in big trouble! To my surprise, they came to my rescue. Without saying a word, they both started to push my twenty-year-old Model-A. Within moments, I was on my way; I was so relieved!

If pushing didn't work, I had to wait for another car to get behind me, bumper to bumper, and give me a push that way. Of course, sometimes none of these tricks seemed to do the job, and before long the prophecy of my car being like a bank was fulfilled. Mechanics didn't work for free. Even though it wasn't cheap to have a vehicle, it did serve me for more than a year. When I returned to class the second year in the fall of 1949, I used my car to take turns going to school in Simcoe with the other fellows.

While many things were relatively primitive in comparison to what we have today, there was always good food on the table. In the 1940s and 1950s, many of the farmers still worked with horses. During harvest time, they worked together, because few of them had enough equipment and manpower to do it on their own. I helped most of the farmers in our community and ate at their table at lunchtime. Often they served chicken, potatoes, and plenty of pie for dessert. Besides a good meal, they paid me $5 to $6 per day. I became acquainted with many new people this way. By the time my year and a half in Port Rowan ended, I knew almost everyone in our church by name.

Back Row: Uncle Jake and Aunt Luise Enns, Aunt Tina and Uncle Geroge Derksen.

Front Row: Cousin Maragaret, unidentified person, Jake, Cousin Hilda.

CHAPTER 18

The Basket Factory in Grimsby

I didn't intend to work on a farm all my life. Since I had little opportunity in the Port Rowan area to secure an industrial job, or to continue my apprenticeship for a future trade, I started to look for something else. I contacted my mother's sister Tina and Uncle George Derksen in Beamsville, near the city of St. Catharines. They took me in for room and board and charged me $10 per week. I lived there from November of 1949 until 1951.

In Beamsville, I had the opportunity to practice my English. While my uncle and aunt spoke mostly German, my five cousins spoke only English to one another and to me. I also continued to take English classes — four years of it altogether.

While I lived at the Derksens, my cousin Margaret was taking piano lessons. One day I asked her to teach me, and she agreed. However, she didn't charge me for it, and I became lax in practicing. That needed to change, so I started taking lessons from the same certified piano teacher as Margaret. I was twenty-three then.

The piano teacher, Mrs. Haste, was an elderly woman in Vineland. I paid fifty cents for a half-hour lesson—one hour's wages in the basket factory. Now I had reason to practice, and I did. I made good progress. She had a beautiful Heintzman piano. I had never heard such a rich sound! I began to dream of owning one for myself someday.

While at the Derksens, I made friends with my cousin Pete, who was a few years younger than I. We both enjoyed skating; he had a pair of skates, but I didn't. One day he sold them to me and bought himself another pair. After that, we often skated together. Later on, after we both married, he joined a pheasant-hunting club. Sometimes I went with him and his dog.

Derksen's oldest daughter Hilda and I started to look for work. We went to many places in St. Catharines. I even applied at the General Motors plant on Ontario Street, then known as McKinnon's. No luck. Finally, we both found work in Grimsby at Farrell's Basket Factory. I worked ten hours a day for fifty cents an hour. We often worked part of the day on Saturday. After deductions, my weekly pay amounted to about $20. With an old car to keep up, and new clothes to buy occasionally, I had little weekly cash left over. However, food was inexpensive— a loaf of bread or a quart of milk cost eighteen cents.

One day I told my aunt about my financial concerns and asked her if we could agree on a little less than $10 per week. After deductions from my weekly pay, that amounted to more than two full days of work. She agreed; from then on, I paid $7 per week.

In Beamsville, I joined the Vineland Mennonite Brethren Church. This was a larger church than the one I had just come from in Port Rowan. There I had gotten to know almost everyone and had connected quickly with people my age; here I felt alone. I had always desired to have a close friend like David and Jonathan, as found in 1 Samuel 18. I prayed that God would connect me with such a person.

Not long after this, like a miracle, I spotted a young man about my age after church. Instantly I *knew* this was the answer to my prayer. I approached him without hesitation. He introduced himself as Hans Kasdorf. He had come from Brazil to study in Canada. He didn't have a car, but I had my old Model-A Ford. I will never forget all the places we went together and how we shared our lives with one another. His sincerity about living the Christian life deeply impressed me.

My friend Hans Kasdorf and I

Our friendship continued for sixty-one years. He visited us several times in Ontario; the last time was on August 17, 1997, with his wife Frieda. Hans wrote in our guest book: "Too late for your birthday, but in time for renewed and extended friendship." It was a visit Kaethe and I will never forget. We also visited him and Frieda at least twice in California; the last time was in 2005. We kept in contact by mail, telephone, and e-mail. *"There is a friend who sticks closer than a brother"* (Proverbs 18:24). He wanted to be the first to purchase a copy of my story. Unfortunately, Hans passed away on March 26, 2011. I flew to Fresno for his memorial service on April 1. Kaethe and I already miss him very much.

Around the age of twenty-three, I decided it would be a good idea to start living on my own. I had been driving ten kilometres a day to my job in Grimsby. It would save me money to live in the same town where I worked. It would also give me the opportunity to do things my own way.

Shortly before moving to Grimsby, I purchased a better car—a 1946 Chevy—formerly owned by the Bell Telephone Company. It was a huge improvement over my Model-A Ford, which I sold for about $100. The Chevy had been repainted shiny black and looked like new. Through the grapevine, I heard some people envied me. I had only been in this new country for about two years and I was already driving a fairly new car.

I lived at several different places in Grimsby—always with Ukrainian families. Once I lived at 101 Main Street West with a family by the name Datskiv. Their house was close to the basket factory where I worked.

At first, I only did manual labour; later I made the actual baskets on a machine. It wasn't hard work, but to make a good wage my hands had to be lightning fast. Later on, I worked on an electric machine that chopped the veneer to size. Several women worked next to me on a table for sorting the veneer. It was a good opportunity to practice my English, because they did a lot of talking—it wasn't always ladylike, either!

The basket factory in Grimsby with my
Model A Ford in the foreground.

I worked for that factory as long as it existed. However, about three o'clock one morning something woke me up from a deep sleep. I noticed that the sky was red. Since I was still quite drowsy, I lay back down to go to sleep. Suddenly, it dawned on me to take a better look. Our factory was on fire! Since I lived so close to it, I noticed sparks dropping on my car in the driveway. I quickly moved it to a safer spot. My place of employment burned to the ground; I was now out of work. Grimsby had a second basket factory near the railway station; I worked there for a short time.

Around this time, I became acquainted with a young Ukrainian man, a carpenter by the name of John Evanetz. He offered me sporadic work at first; later he employed me full-time. He built new homes, renovated older ones, and did fine woodworking, such as making jewellery boxes and carvings. From him, I gained experience in everything related to building houses — pouring footings, doing concrete work, framing, shingling, siding, and doing finish carpentry.

Finish carpentry interested me most; it became my occupation for more than three decades. However, in the fall of 1952, I decided to go to Bible school in Niagara-on-the-Lake. While I was familiar with Scripture, I realized I could learn more. I also continued my piano lessons there and spent many hours practicing. My school marks surprised me; I ended the year with an average of 86%.

The school published a yearbook at the end of the year with a photo of each student. Someone chose the following rhyme to place under my photo: "He is at the piano, or else he's reading—anxious to follow his Master's leading." Yes, this uplifted and encouraged me. It's still my goal to live this way.

CHAPTER 19

Carpentry in St. Catharines

After the school year was over in 1953, I needed a place to stay. Someone told me about the Peter Schmidts and their teenage son Walter, whom I knew from Russia. Mrs. Schmidt was my mother's close friend. The family now lived in St. Catharines, so I contacted them to see if they would consider having me stay with them for room and board. They consented and I lived with them for the next four years.

Since their house was small and they already had a married couple living with them, they made the sunroom into a bedroom for me. They charged me a reasonable price. Later, when the married couple moved out, they gave me one of their bedrooms. With better accommodation, the price for my stay also went up.

I had now accomplished two of my three goals: I had learned English, and I owned a good vehicle. All I needed was a telephone. The Schmidts didn't have one, but they allowed me to have one installed.

A couple of years earlier, I had purchased an old piano and had moved it numerous times. The Schmidts allowed me to bring it with me. We placed it in their living room, where it stayed for four years.

I found employment as a finish carpenter under two partners, Peter Huebert and Peter Becker. I started to work for a moderate hourly wage. However, when they noticed my skills and observed my performance, they soon gave me a pay raise without me asking for it. While their motives might not have been altogether due to generosity, they soon realized that if they didn't treat a good worker fairly, he might look elsewhere for work. While it was never my practice to hop from job to job, my employers knew this could happen.

Peter Becker immigrated to Canada about the same time as I did, whereas Peter Huebert had grown up in Canada. He and his parents had immigrated to Germany before the war, and returned to Canada after it was over. Therefore, he spoke fluent German. He had a good vocabulary, but some of his grammar was often incorrect. I often found it difficult to listen to it without correcting him; his partner wasn't any better.

One thing in particular that always hurt my ears was when they confused the words *dir* and *dich*, or *mir* and *mich*. For example, they would say, *"Heute komme ich zu dich, und morgen kommst du zu mich."* One day I finally found the courage to say, "One doesn't say, *'Ich komme zu dich oder du kommst zu mich.'* One says, *'Ich komme zu dir und du kommst zu mir!'"*

Whereupon, Peter Huebert said, *"Ja, ob nun zu mir oder zu mich, das bleibt sich mich gleich, aber deins und meins, das ist ein Unterschied!"* ("It makes no difference if you say *'zu mir'* or *'zu mich,'* but when it comes to *yours* or *mine*, there *is* a difference!") You just couldn't win.

Other than that, I got along quite well with them.

One day, they told me they planned to go into house construction as general contractors. They asked me if I would like to take on their finish carpentry business and I accepted their offer. Thus, I began sub-contracting for Bartlett Builders, one of the largest builders in St. Catharines.

I realized that working on my own meant I would need my own tools. I had most of the hand tools, but no table saw, the most important power tool for the trade. I purchased a brand new one. As I brought it into the house for the first time, Peter Becker took one look at it, then glanced at his older saw nearby. I smiled and said in a joking way, *"En wone ack well jie june soag habe?"* ("In which corner would you like to have your table saw?") He understood the joke, turned to his partner, and said, *"Weisst du was er eben sagte?"* ("Do you know what he just said?") In a low voice he repeated what I had asked, emphasizing each word in High German: *"In... welche... Ecke... wollt... Ihr... eure... Saege... haben?"* All three of us had a good laugh.

In the early 1950s, the economy was booming. Mr. Bartlett built so many houses that he needed three to four crews of finish carpenters; I was one of them. Mr. Bartlett was a good man to do business with—a Christian and an honest person. I always knew that when I finished a job well, a cheque would soon follow.

Shortly before I began subcontracting, I traded in my 1946 Chevy for a brand new half-ton Chevy pickup truck. It was something else! I saw it in the showroom window at the Crews Chevy-Oldsmobile dealership on Ontario Street. It was better equipped than any I had ever seen. It was bright red with a white top and white-wall tires. The box had a zipped blue tarp to close the back. It had benches in the back and a high-gloss oak floor. The hood ornament was a flying jet; the interior was red and white leather. It turned heads when I drove along St. Paul Street. I took good care of it, as I did with everything I owned and worked for, and kept it for eleven years. When I finally sold it, it still looked almost like new. I was amazed when I passed it on the road once thirty-five to forty years later!

My 1953 pickup!

Soon after I started subcontracting, I found a young man named Henry Hahn who was willing to work for me. In German, the name Hahn means rooster. Obviously, those of us who spoke German loved to tease him, especially during lunch hour. However, this "rooster" was clever and not easily offended. One day, a group of five or six of us was having lunch together when we noticed he was looking at the ceiling with his head tilted sideways. Someone asked, "Well, Rooster, what are you looking for?"

"I'm looking for a two-by-four close to the ceiling where I can sit and eat my grain," he said.

Everyone had a good laugh!

Soon I needed more helpers. One day, a friend asked me for a job. Knowing that carpentry wasn't his greatest gift, I asked, "What can you do?"

"I can straighten out crooked nails. How much will you pay?"

"I'll give you half the nails you straighten out," I answered. I said it in good humour, but he got the message; he never asked me for work again.

As time went on, I hired other workers—many of them with little experience in woodworking. I spent much time training them. As a subcontractor, I was fully responsible for delivering quality workmanship. I did it not only to get paid, but also because my Christian parents had taught me to always do the best job possible. I tried to obey the Scriptures, which say, *"Not by way of eyeservice, as men-pleasers, but as slaves of Christ, doing the will of God from the heart"* (Ephesians 6:6).

Delivering quality workmanship became my deep conviction; it was more than a duty. When everyone had gone home after work, I spent another ten to fifteen minutes checking the work throughout the house, making sure it was done well. Unfortunately, not everyone working for me had the same ethics. When I paid by the hour, some produced little; I lost more than I gained by keeping such workers. In 1956, the Industrial Standard Act introduced a new law increasing the minimum wage to $2.05 an hour for our industry. Impossible! That would mean paying more than what I received from the contractor. After that, I decided to pay what was called "piecework," or according to how much they produced.

That created another problem. Many were eager to produce a lot, but they didn't care about the quality of their workmanship. Not surprisingly, I sometimes felt it necessary to ask some of the employees to redo their work without additional pay. As a subcontractor, I was responsible to the general contractor and the prospective purchaser of the house, who wouldn't accept poor workmanship. My new policy paid off. Numerous other subcontractors soon paid their employees piecework as well.

Good workmanship, dependability, conscientious-
ness, and organization always yield good results. Since
my business wasn't large enough to have a secretary, I
did all of the bookwork myself. In the 1950s and 1960s,
every employer had to purchase unemployment insur-
ance stamps and paste them into a booklet for each employee. The government required me to have my books
checked once a year to see if they conformed to their
regulations.

On one occasion, the official claimed some stamps
were missing and I had to pay the missing amount. I
couldn't believe it. I was so careful and conscientious.
However, since it wasn't a large sum of money, I decided
to pay it. I made it a point to be doubly careful in the
future.

The same thing happened the next year. Since I was
busy and didn't want to spend a lot of time proving
them wrong, I simply paid the requested amount again.
As unbelievable as it may sound, it happened a third
time. This time I decided, "Enough is enough." I took
my books to the officer in charge and asked for proof
of his claim. When he finished checking my books, he
found them to be in order, without any error.

He then began to make comparisons between my
records and those of other employers—how messy and

confusing some of them were. He said, "Your books are organized and in proper order." He continued to make complimentary comments about my bookkeeping. Before I left his office, he said it again—the third time. Not only did his compliments make me feel good, but he also refunded the entire amount charged prior to the investigation.

My employees and I seldom lacked work. Yes, there were lean periods, but we were usually busy, even while others were looking for work in winter and early spring. Besides this, throughout the years numerous builders and their customers sent me compliments and words of appreciation for work well done, some of them in writing. I attribute this to the teaching of my godly parents. I truly believe our Christian beliefs need to be demonstrated in our daily performance.

I have to confess that I didn't talk about my faith on the job very often, unless the proper opportunity arose. For example, one day a builder came into the house where we were working. Immediately, he came to me and asked, "Jake, will you pray for me?" I said, "Yes," thinking I would pray for him when I arrived home that night.

However, that's not what he had in mind. The moment I said, "Yes," he grabbed my hand and took me to another room to pray. I was barely able to collect my thoughts and ask, "What would you like me to pray for?" He told me, and we both knelt and prayed, asking the Lord to meet his need. After we finished, I invited him to a Christian meeting a few days from then. He not only showed up, but also responded to the altar call. He gave his heart to the Lord that very night.

This man experienced a transformation that reminded me of the Apostle Paul on the way to Damascus. He changed his membership from an orthodox church to an evangelical fellowship. He also became a brother and a friend. From time to time, we met together after that. My wife and I also visited him in his home shortly before he passed away.

CHAPTER 20

Making a House into a
Home with Kaethe

I was twenty-five years old in 1953 when I went to live with the Schmidts. During my four years with them, I worked full-time and saved some money. I wanted to build a house, get married, and have a family of my own. While living there, I also changed my membership from the Vineland to the Scott Street Mennonite Brethren Church in St. Catharines.

I began to think seriously about finding a life partner; I was choosier than some others in this matter. Yes, I had opportunities. Some girls let me know of their availability; more than one mother even made it clear she would like to become my future mother-in-law. However, I didn't find the one who was right for me. I began to pray for God's guidance. I realized the importance of having a life partner approved by the Lord.

One day, I talked with my friends Peter and Mary Friesen, whom I had assisted to emigrate from Paraguay to Canada. One day they showed me photos of students and teachers in Paraguay. I spotted a good-looking young girl and asked, "Who is this girl? Does she have a boyfriend?" They said they didn't think so. I asked Mary if she would write to this "cutie," Kaethe Duerksen, and find out if she would allow me to correspond with her. She was willing! However, by the second or third letter, I realized she wasn't ready to be swept off her feet just yet. I took the hint, but continued to correspond.

Kaethe Duerksen (front centre) caught my eye!

I had known her Uncle Martin, her father's younger brother and his family, for a few years and thought highly of them. Therefore, I thought this could also be a good family. I decided to talk this matter over with a highly respected minister, Rev. C.C. Peters, who had been Kaethe's instructor in teacher's college for two years in Paraguay. When I asked him about Kaethe, he said, *"Sie ist eine gesunde, starke Jungfrau, wirb um ihre Hand!"* ("She's a healthy and strong young lady. Go for it!") Those words encouraged me to continue what I had begun.

Kaethe's parents and two of her sisters immigrated to Canada in 1955. When Kaethe and her two siblings arrived in January of 1956, I went to meet her. She was not only good-looking, but also bright and intelligent. She introduced me to her younger sisters, whom she seemed to be very proud of. I felt I had chosen the best. I still believe this after more than fifty years of marriage.

Shortly after this first meeting, Kaethe invited me to meet her family. I was impressed by how they communicated with one another. Their home was filled with love, kindness, and respect for one another. I wondered if I would be able to measure up. They treated me kindly, and I tried my best to do the same. Kaethe and I soon met on a regular basis. She was twenty-five and I was twenty-eight. As time went on, we became better acquainted.

Kaethe's siblings in 1994 - Front: Peter, Mary, Jake.
Back: Kaethe, Susie, Agatha, Elisabeth, Margaret.

One day I asked her the important question: "Will you marry me?" I didn't get a definite "yes" the first time, but I realized it didn't mean "no" either. I didn't push her; I wanted to be sure she agreed.

As the weather warmed up, I took her on Sundays in my pickup to Niagara Falls, Fort Erie, Toronto, Casa-Loma, and many other places. We never went to places where we couldn't return home the same day. After dating this way for several months, I asked her again to marry me. This time she said yes!

According to tradition, I had to ask Kaethe's parents for their consent. She arranged a day for us to meet with them. After I told them briefly about the decision Kaethe and I had made, I asked for their consent. They didn't jump to their feet shouting, "Halleluiah!" I did hear her mother whisper, *"Wada jewe."* ("Giving again," as this was the fourth child they had given away in marriage.) However, they both agreed without hesitation, whereupon her father suggested we bring this matter to the Lord in prayer—a meaningful new beginning.

Sadly, her father passed away much too soon. I would have loved to get to know him better and spend more time with him. Unfortunately, the unbearable conditions in the Paraguayan Chaco and a second settlement in Friesland robbed him of his health. As a result, after living only two years in Canada, he passed away at the age of sixty.

We decided to celebrate our engagement, as was the custom. We invited Rev. Isaak Loewen and his wife, whom I had gotten to know in Germany. He used the text: *"I will betroth you to Me forever; Yes, I will betroth you to Me in righteousness and in justice, in lovingkindness and in compassion"* (Hosea 2:19). It was a cherished time with only Kaethe's parents, the Loewens, Kaethe, and me.

The day after our engagement
Left: Kaethe's Uncle Martin and Aunt Justina Durksen.
Right: Kaethe's parents, Peter and Agatha Duerksen.
Kaethe and Jake are in the centre surrounded by family members.

That was in November of 1956—the same day I hired a bulldozer to dig the basement for the "castle" I was about to build. I mainly hired sub-trades to do the construction while I supervised. We decided our wedding would take place on April 6, 1957. My goal was to have the house ready for us to move into by that date.

On our wedding day, we had rain mixed with snow, but there would be many nice days ahead of us. The day was a highlight for Kaethe and me. Kaethe's mother had recently lost her husband due to his illness. I heard

Kaethe and I on our wedding day

people speak comforting and encouraging words to her that day.

By now, I had saved enough money to pay for the lot and about half the cost of building our new house. I took a loan for the balance—to be paid off in ten years. I kept enough cash to buy a fridge, stove, dining room set, bedroom suite, sofa and chair, and all the kitchen utensils.

We moved into our new home immediately after the wedding. We had agreed not to take a long trip, as most couples did. I felt it was more important to look after the basics first—traveling could come later, and it did. However, I did rent a 1957 Pontiac for several days. For our honeymoon, we decided to go to one of the world's most favourite and famous places for newlyweds. Yes, we made a trip to the "Honeymoon Capital of the World"—Niagara Falls. Like any newly married couple, we loved each other and spent several days together before I returned to work.

Shortly before the wedding, I finished all the carpentry in our house. Kaethe had helped me with the painting and staining. After the wedding, however, there wasn't much for Kaethe to do. We didn't have a garden, lawn, or even flowers to take care of. I grew up with the understanding that wives stayed home and did the housework, and didn't work in a factory or office. It never entered my mind to send her out to find a job. Providing for the family was the husband's responsibility, in spite of the fact that I knew many women were working outside of the home. At first, Kaethe felt lonely in our "big house," as she referred to it. Sometimes she asked to come along to my workplace. She watched me work or read a book, which she always loved to do.

CHAPTER 21

Our Family Grows to Six

Our first son was born on February 4, 1958; we named him Helmut. Kaethe had a difficult time, as he had to be delivered by Caesarean section. She felt weak for some time after the delivery, but her spirit remained strong and positive.

When I picked Kaethe and our newborn son up from the hospital, we also brought her mother along. When we arrived home, Kaethe's mother was holding the baby and was about to carry him into the house. She wanted me to carry the diaper bag! Without saying a word, I took my son out of her arms and carried him into my "castle."

Our second son, Walter, was born on May 28, 1959. Siegfried arrived September 20, 1961. Our youngest, Peter, entered our family on November 22, 1963. All four were delivered by Caesarean section. It was indeed difficult for Kaethe, even though I helped her as much as I could. She deserves to be congratulated. Kaethe's mother loved the children; we felt good about leaving them in her care when we left on a trip or for business out of town.

We certainly were blessed with our four sons. Helmut, our oldest, was a good-looking baby and healthy child. When he learned to talk, he asked many, many questions, especially of his mother, since she was at home with him. He investigated everything in the house. To keep him safe, I had to put locks on every door and drawer. However, at the age of three, he reached up to the kitchen counter, grabbed a bowl of hot gravy, and dumped it on his face and chest; the scars remained for the rest of his life.

By Grade One, I noticed his insatiable desire to read everything he saw. As we drove to town, he would read every sign and number in sight. Because he read out loud, I knew he was reading what was actually written. At first I thought, "What a little show-off!" Of course, I never told him that. After he grew older, he loved to read—to the point where we almost had to force him to go outside and play with the other children.

I had quite a few books on my bookshelves. One day when he was a teenager, I searched for one of my books and couldn't find it. Finally, it occurred to me to check Helmut's bookshelves in his room. I not only found the one I was looking for, but more than forty others!

He showed an interest in playing the beautiful Heintzman piano I owned. I found some early lesson books and he became my first piano student. He learned quickly. Within a few years, he was able to play almost anything, even classical music. I could have become *his* student, even though I had completed grade eight piano lessons and had taken one year of classical music. Later on, he also learned to play the recorder.

Helmut always received the highest marks in school—usually in the eighties and nineties. Sadly, during his late teenage years, we watched his behaviour and thinking change with the onset of schizophrenia. This became extremely difficult for him and our whole family.

Because he loved books and school, he decided to live in Kitchener-Waterloo, close to the universities. He tried many times to take some courses, but he couldn't seem to make progress. He spent much time in hospitals—in Kitchener, London, and St. Catharines. As parents, we tried our utmost to help him. Anytime he called us, we left everything and went to see him. After battling this disease for more than twenty years, his life came to a tragic end on September 24, 2001. What a loss!

Helmut

Walter, our second son, was also a handsome and healthy boy. He wasn't as much into reading as Helmut, but as he grew older it became evident that he had abilities in more practical areas. He took an interest in mechanical and electrical projects. He liked to take things apart and put them back together again. In his teen years, he showed great interest in science, technology, aerodynamics, and astronomy. He often amazed me with his knowledge and understanding.

He was fanatical about driving cars. I'll never forget taking him on the road for the first time. He handled the vehicle as if he had done it all his life. When I expressed my amazement at his excellent performance, he looked at me with a smirk on his face and asked, "Didn't you know I was born with a wheel in my hands?"

Years later, in1991, our garage roof began to sag. The pressure of the roof caused the rear wall to bow. I realized this would only get worse if not repaired. One day as I was talking to Walter, I told him I was planning to buy a chain to fasten the front wall to the back wall to keep it from bowing any further.

He gave me a funny look, nudged my shoulder, and said, "Dad, why don't you do something that makes sense?"

"What do you mean?" I asked.

He then came up with a brilliant idea. Our house was a story and a half with a steep roof, bedrooms on the second floor, and a garage six feet away from the house. The front wall of the garage was in line with the front wall of the house. He said, "Why don't you take the roof off of the garage, bring it in line with the roof of the house, and attach the two? Add some dormers over the garage and the breezeway; this will give you a second floor over the garage. It will make the house more saleable in the future."

The moment I heard him say this, it made a lot of sense. I looked into the situation. Would adding 650 square feet of living space increase our taxes? City hall assured me it wouldn't, if the space remained unfinished. We did make the changes, as our clever son had suggested. Several neighbours came and complimented our new residence. One of them said our house was the nicest looking one on our street.

Our third son, Siegfried, weighed the most at birth, but had much less hair than his older brothers. When he first started school, he had problems pronouncing certain words correctly. Instead of saying "city hall," he said "shitty hall." After speech therapy with a good

Sieg demonstrating his talents!

teacher, he learned to speak properly. However, every so often someone in the family would remind him of that old "shitty hall." He accepted the ribbing in a good-natured way.

Later in childhood, he created and demonstrated the most humorous acts and plays. One day, he and Walter were playing in the backyard. They used KFC buckets for helmets and cut a couple of holes in them to see through. Each had a huge "sword" for this imaginary battle. They had a hilarious time! Another time he took an empty mesh orange bag, pulled it over his head, and flattened his nose and face with it. Not only did *he* enjoy himself, but *we* had fun watching him.

When Sieg was eighteen, he went west to work in Alberta. After several years there, he returned to Ontario. I sensed he wanted to work for me again, but I was thinking more about retiring than hiring. I suggested he work for his older brother Walter, which he did. However, he soon came back and asked to work for me again. After some consideration, I agreed. He worked for me for as long as work was available.

In 1991, when work was slow, Kaethe and I planned a trip to Germany. When we returned, I told Sieg, "I'll let you have whatever work there is. I've wanted a sabbatical anyway."

Watler and Sieg having fun (our swing is in the background)

Peter and Sieg clowning around (Helmut is in the background)

Around this time, Sieg asked me if we could build houses together. I wasn't interested, since I had done that before and knew the risks and headaches connected with it. However, since he was my son, and because I knew he didn't have the finances to buy construction lots and building materials, I agreed. We built a couple of houses as partners, but I soon turned the business over to him. I gave him my good-looking pickup with the home-built box to use for his work.

At age twenty-seven, Sieg married a beautiful young Christian girl, Karen Stone. He was the first to get married, even though he was the second youngest. Several years later, they made us grandparents. We thank God for him, Karen and their three children, Alastair, Audra, and Adrianna.

Siegfried and Karen's family in 2010: Audra, Alastair, and Adrianna

A few years ago, Sieg said, "I always thought I was your favourite son." While I had tried to treat my children equally, it felt good to hear him say that. It proved to Kaethe and me that he felt loved in our family. Perhaps this feeling of being loved, accepted, and allowed to be who he really was had something to do with his natural inclination to be humorous.

Sieg now has his own carpentry business and is doing well. Karen operates a daycare centre; she loves her work, and the children love her. They live close by, so we visit back and forth. We are so proud of both of them; we love them and their children.

My first recollection of Peter is hearing him cry in the next room as I was standing beside Kaethe's bed in the hospital with the nurse beside me, saying, "That's your son!" I'll never forget that soft, tender wail. It touched my heart as nothing had ever done before. I felt love welling up inside of me, and a bonding like no other. It still moves me to tears as I write this. I felt the same love for my wife Kaethe, who went through so much pain and suffering to have a family. I love her more than anyone.

Peter was a sweet little fellow. He was always slim—not as robust as many boys. He readily gave and received love from others. Often he sat on my lap and put his head against my shoulder; it made both of us feel so good, like a little kitten purring on my lap!

I still remember him leaving for school the first day. As he walked down the driveway, he turned around, smiled, and waved good-bye in such a way that it looked as if he had been trained for a perfect performance. I could almost see a future actor in this boy.

When he was about six, our family was invited to attend a neighbour's church. At the beginning of the service, a woman asked all the children up to a certain age to come join her for a Sunday school class. About thirty minutes later, he tromped back in with a big grin on his face. While still several metres away, he said, "That was kid's stuff!"

Our "quartet" on Peter's first day of school.

I whispered, "Shhh, you don't say that."

He behaved and didn't say another word about that—in the church anyway.

However, when we arrived home, he sat next to me at lunchtime and said with a smirk on his face, "Dad, the Sunday school teacher was swearing."

"What did she say?"

"I don't want to say it."

Now I became curious and wondered what in the world might have happened to provoke the teacher to swear. I said a second time, "Peter, it's okay. You can tell me."

He shook his head and still refused to say anything.

However, I realized he was itching to tell me. Now I began to itch! I realized he wouldn't say anything because he didn't want to repeat bad language.

"Peter, you can tell me what the teacher said," I told him. "You will still go to heaven. If there's going to be any problem, I'll take responsibility for it."

With obvious relief, he said, "Well, she was asking questions, and nobody knew the answer except me. Every time she asked a question, up went my hand! Then she said, 'Holy crow! We've got a smart kid in our class!'"

I still laugh every time I tell this story.

One day when Peter was about four years old and Sieg was six, they were sitting on the floor in my office, squabbling about something. My mind was occupied with paperwork when I suddenly heard them discussing a painting on the wall. Their mother had made this black and white pen drawing (*Federstrich-zeichnung*) for me. She had learned the art while in teacher's college in South America.

I heard Peter say, "I don't like that picture."

Sieg said, "It's not so bad."

"This is *not* a nice picture," Peter kept saying.

Sieg finally had enough of that. "But Peter, you also have to remember, in those days, they didn't have the education *we* have now."

When Peter was about fourteen, we were all sitting around the table when the boys discussed the meaning of their names. The oldest three each managed to come up with an interpretation. Each tried to outdo the other as to the importance of *his* name. Because Peter was unable to come up with an interpretation, the others began to tease him, saying he was less important. It was all done in good humour. All of a sudden, Peter ran upstairs to his room and promptly returned with an interpretation for *his* name: "P stands for perfect, E for excellent, T for terrific, E for enthusiastic, and R for righteous." No one could beat that!

When Peter was twenty-four, he was the only one still living at home. As it is with most young people at that age, the grass looked greener on the other side of the fence; Peter was no exception. He rented a room in someone's basement in Vineland. We helped him move and, for a little while, he seemed to be doing all right. Before long, however, he started coming back to our house for a good meal and sunbathing on our lawn, which he always loved to do.

One day, he asked me, "Are you interested in having someone in your house for room and board?"

Knowing what he wanted even before he finished the question, I said, "Well, if anyone is interested, we operate by the principle 'first come, first served.' We would consider receiving an application."

Not long after that, he came over again for dinner. Kaethe and I had planned to eat out that evening. Before we left, I said, "If you want any raspberries, pick as many as you like. You can also eat anything on the table, or take it with you."

When we came home, he was gone, but he had filled our bedroom and kitchen with balloons. He left the following note on the table, dated July 11, 1987:

Dear Mom and Dad,

Thank you both for two terrific days! Thanks, too, for the baked goods! I hereby submit my application for permanent residence.

Peter

I still have this note in my files, along with many others.

One day we received the good news that Peter wanted to get married. He had found a lovely Christian girl named Kathy Wichert. Kaethe and I were so proud of his choice. We knew Kathy came from a good family; she was the daughter of his former high school teacher, Jake Wichert.

They married in 1991, and are doing well. For the last ten years or more, they have made their home in Charlotte, North Carolina, where Peter works for the Bank of America. They have four healthy children: Jessica, Bennett, Sydney Grace, and Nathan. They love every one of them, and so do we. A number of years ago, Peter went back to school to further his education; he graduated from the University of North Carolina with a B.A. degree. After that, he also graduated from a theological seminary with a master's degree in psychology.

Kathy has a good education, too. She is an excellent pianist and gives piano lessons to children. She's a good housekeeper and isn't afraid to get her hands dirty planting flowers and vegetables.

Peter's family. Standing: Sydney Grace, Jessica, Bennett and Nathan. Seated: Peter and Kathy.

CHAPTER 22

Treasured Notes from the Boys

Kaethe and I have kept a stack of notes the boys have written to us over the years. I would like to share some of these "treasures" with you. The love we showed to them was returned a thousand-fold.

Helmut's Notes

August 9, 1971:

I am very thankful that Dad cares for us. When he comes home, many times he has something good to eat. Dad takes time to play games and also takes us on enjoyable vacation trips. I think that in teaching and training us he is success-ful. Working with Dad is fun. I am glad we have such a loving father. Helmut (13 years old).

Dᴇꜱ 25. 1978

To the head of the household and his partner
We are grateful to you for opening your home to us
four strangers. It has been rewarding to come to
know each other. The food was great and the fellowship
enriching. Thank-you for your hospitality. You have
put Hebrews 13 2 into practice! "Do not neglect
to show hospitality to strangers, for by this some
have entertained angels without knowing it. We
hope that we will continue to be welcome in
this home. Love Peter, Lucy, Helmut, Walter

Note found in guest book

April 6, 1978:

Dear Dad and Mom, I just want to congratulate you on arriving at your 21st anniversary with flying colors! I think it's great to have parents, which take time to talk and listen to their children. I appreciate it very much when we can sit down and discuss various topics. It has often happened that I've been really encouraged to grow closer to the Lord, and to seek His will, through one of our talks. And at a time of life when the future seems so unsure, that really makes life right now worth living. Love, your son, Helmut (20 years old).

*   *   *

December 25, 1978:

Dear Dad and Mom, To put my feelings into words is not easy. It is difficult to express what you mean to me, but I will try. When a young person senses that the two people who brought him into the word love him, he feels secure. When he can share his concerns and ideas freely, he is deeply encouraged. When he becomes convinced that they believe in him, he grows so strong that, despite all his weaknesses, he feels he can face the whole world. I know, because I am experiencing these things. For this, I offer you my thanks.

When a Christian discovers fellowship in his own home, he has something to offer other people. When he can see his parents growing, he realizes that a relationship with God can never stand still. When he can pray with Dad and Mom, he begins to see how precious it is to belong to the family of God. I know, because I also experience these things. For this, I offer

Him my thanks. With all my love, your son, Helmut (20 years old).

*   *   *

Dear Dad and Mom, The more I get to know other people, the more I realize how fortunate I am to have a home like ours. Your love for us is obvious in the way you spend so much time and energy in developing good relationships.

Dad: I am thankful for you because you are really concerned about bringing us up the right way— and that you do something about it.

Mom: Thank you for choosing to be a "woman who fears the Lord," and showing it every day.

God bless you both, Helmut (about 25 years old).

*   *   *

August 9, 1987:

Yesterday was your 60th birthday. This is a milestone in your life, and I have been thinking about this event for several months. The first thought was that my Dad turning sixty is unbelievable. And immediately this feeling arises: "How dare you grow old before my very eyes?" (And then I remember that I myself will turn thirty in six months…)

Most of all I became troubled this week that I could think of nothing to give you on your birthday. I feel ashamed that I might come home empty-handed, with no gift for you. Behind all these worries lies my love for you. I have come to realize that I am a person who feels intensely…

Would you tell me what really happened in the war?

Please be assured of my deep love for you, Dad. I wish you many more years to enjoy yourself, Mom, and perhaps even some grand-children! I know you'd make a good grand-father, just as you've been a good father. I mean that. Your son, Helmut (29 years old).

* * *

Helmut, we miss you. I know you would have enjoyed reading my book!

Monday, July 10, 1995:

Thank you for your gestures of support, particularly at my bedside in the St. Joseph's Emergency Department while awaiting my treatment. Do not underestimate the value of your caring hands at that critical time! Dad, I especially treasure the memory of your gentle words to me about my hands being as warm as my heart is. You could only know this through being through it yourself, as well. I am receiving excellent treatment here in London... .So, to sum up, I thank you for your care for me. I am in caring hands here... Love, Helmut (37 years old).

*　　*　　*

Walter's Notes

Here is a Valentine's card from 1967:

I'd be a square not to want you! To Father, from Walter B. (8 years old)

*　　*　　*

August 8, 1971:

Dear Dad, I would like to tell you some of the things I like about you. I think it was a good idea to have the Bible clubs in our home, and I enjoyed it. I also like going on vacation, because we had a lot of fun together. I thank you for your care and everything else. Love, Walter (12 years old).

Drawing by Walter, age 11

Another drawing by Walter, age 11

Walter in foreground, left, with his cousins.

Siegfried's Notes

August 8, 1971:

Dear Dad, I thank you for giving me things like toys and food and clothes. I like going on trips with you. You love me and keep me alive. You do many good things for me, and do things right. From, Sieg (10 years old).

*   *   *

I love you because you don't spoil me, you love me, give me enough to eat, discipline me, and take time for me. Some improvements I'd like to see are, be more strict. When you are old, I

will give you extra money and take care of you.
Love, Siegfried (about 10 years old).

*   *   *

Siegfried wrote the following note while I was on my first trip to Germany with Peter Friesen in July 1973:

Dear Dad, I already miss you. I'm "Dad sick."
I just about started to cry when you left. Things
are still going all right around here. I love you,
Sieg.

*   *   *

And then, a little later:

I hope you are enjoying your vacation vastly.
Have you seen any dykes yet? (Don't forget
to send the cards each day you promised!) We
hope we get some news from you soon. Sieg (12
years old).

*   *   *

The following are excerpts from letters Sieg wrote from Calgary, where he worked for several years.

April 19, 1982: …I feel our home was an ex-
cellent place to bring us up… Love, your son,
Sieg (21 years old).

*   *   *

April 26, 1983:

My dear Mom and Dad, I hope you both know that I love you and appreciate you, too. I appreciate that you're genuinely concerned for my welfare... I thank God that your prayers have protected me from these life-changing sins. Sieg (22 years old).

*   *   *

September 26, 1983:

Mom, I really love your outreach ministry. Your sharing Jesus with people you work with is something I can really learn from. Sieg (22 years old).

*   *   *

November 27, 1983:

Dear Mom and Dad, Don't worry; I think you did a great job of raising us. When I read how great men like Eli and Samuel, or even David, raised their sons, and the lives the sons led, I've really got to hand it to you. I've been impressed that though raising a child is done with individual actions, it's the broader "direction" which leaves the impact. If the parents are honestly doing their best in all good conscience, then it's impossible to go wrong in any major way. So, as a self-observed product of your efforts—you did a good job! Thanks. See you soon. Sieg (22 years old).

*   *   *

Kaethe and I took a train trip to B.C. and offered Sieg a ticket from Calgary, where he lived at that time, to Vancouver.

December 26, 1983:

I'm really looking forward to the trip to the coast. That will be an experience that I know will be enjoyable. Of course, it can't be as beautiful as celebrating Christmas together, but it will just have to do. So, thanks for sponsoring the trip (via train) and I'll see you then. Sieg (22 years old).

*   *   *

February 25, 1984:

Dear Mom and Dad, Thanks for your prayers and keep on doing it. Not that I necessarily sell my car, but that I finally find God's will… In love, Sieg (23 years old).

*   *   *

Peter's Notes

August 8, 1971:

*Dear Dad, May this card bring you happiness.
I love you very much, because you give us toys
for Christmas. Some fathers don't give their
children any toys. You're one of the best dads.
Because you are kind, I will do the mail and
newspaper. Love from Peter (8 years old).*

*   *   *

December 1971:

*Dear Dad, I wish you a Merry Christmas. I
remember when you said that you got only one
present in Russia and I felt very sorry for you.
I am very, very, very thankful to you for giving me all sorts of presents on Christmas day.
Thank you for giving me all sorts of presents
even when it is not Christmas. I wish you a
very Merry Christmas. Love, Peter (8 years
old).*

*   *   *

March 31,1973:

Thanks Dad! You and I have had many happy times together. We will have more of them, too. Love, Peter (10 years old).

*   *   *

During my trip to Germany in July 1973:

Five weeks — that is too long! As soon as Daddy will be home, I will forget about my special present and I will hug and kiss him, hug and kiss him, hug and kiss him until Daddy will say, "Now, it's enough Peter. Now it's Sieg's turn." Peter (10 years old).

*   *   *

April 6, 1975:

Dear Mom and Dad, How do you like the drawing? (Self-made picture of Mom and Dad facing one another with a bunch of hearts above the heads) Happy Anniversary, from Sieg and me. Each night I think about what it would be like without parents. Life would be drab. Therefore, I would like to say "Thank you for marrying each other. You make a perfect match." With love, Peter Braun (12 years old).

*   *   *

December 25, 1976:

To the parents whom I am thankful for, who have led me along the narrow path, who have taught me to love God more and more. Thank you. Lovingly, your son Peter (13 years old).

*   *   *

December 25, 1986:

Dear Mom and Dad, I have, of late (hopefully, not too late), become appreciative of what I've learned at home, namely that things worth having are worth sacrificing for. You can probably guess that, for me, that's a big thing. All the while, I remind myself to trust in the Lord with all my heart. "Lean not unto thine own understanding, in all thy ways acknowledge Him, and He will direct thy paths." Have a wonderful Christmas. In love, Peter (23 years old)

*   *   *

The following are excerpts from a letter written in Hawaii.

April 27, 1991:

Dear Mom and Dad, I give thanks for the home the Lord has blessed me with. I really hope that the two of you will get a chance to visit here not too long after Kath and I are settled in together... It is good for me to read how good you, Mom, feel when you think about Kath's and my future...

You know the German plaque you have on the wall in the kitchen above the hallway door? "Bewahret einander vor Herzeleid, kurz ist die Zeit die Ihr beisammen seid..." ("Be sure you do not hurt one another, realizing the time is short that you will be together...") I have loved that one for about as long as I understood its meaning. I'd rather not wait to inherit that one... If you are really attached to it, it belongs on your wall, but in a way, I almost have the nerve to ask you for it for our wedding, so I can hang it above our kitchen door... Little things like that, that continue from one generation to the next, are significant for me.

The other thing that would make my heart happy is something of yours, Dad, creativity with wood. I was almost awed by the beauty of the cabinet you made for the living room, because of its beauty, certainly, but also because it is the fruit of your abilities with wood. Things that are a reflection of a person's talents are always cherished by me… So you have another set of parents, Mom! I think it's great how you fulfill all different kinds of people's needs where you work…

With much aloha, Peter (28 years old).

*   *   *

February 7, 1992:

Dear Mom and Dad, Well! Quite a letter I got yesterday! Your gift of $$$ was as appreciated as it was unexpected!… Your letter, Dad, was quite amusing! I had a chuckle or two as I read it on route to the elementary school where I tutor the fourth graders… Peter (29 years old).

*   *   *

October 24, 1994:

Dear Mom and Dad, Kath and I just wanted to write to you a short note to express our appreciation for all the things you did for us during your visit here. Every time you visit, you seem to bless us in many different ways, and this visit was no exception. Whether it's the cellular phone, the wonderful cooking (and freedom from cooking!), the canned goods and other food gifts, the day of discovery place, the gift for our church, it's all noticed and appreciated! Thank you for all your kindness!

See you at Christmas! In love, Peter and Kathy (Peter, 31 years old).

*   *   *

January 30, 2000:

Hello Dad! I just wanted to send you a picture of the box you made for me, and show you where it sits. It's everything I wanted in a box made by your hands, and it has given me great pleasure to show it off to Hugo and Lydia and many others. Thank you so much for all the work and love you poured into this special creation of yours. It's a treasure! Love, Peter (37 years old).

CHAPTER 23

Our Home on Gregory Road

One Sunday in the summer of 1964, we saw a car turn around on our driveway, back up, and knock over our mailbox. The driver immediately took off in a cloud of dust. He turned into a driveway a few houses from our home.

I decided to look him up and have a talk with him about his cowardly behaviour. As I approached, I said, "Excuse me, sir. Did you knock down our mailbox?"

He said, "Hmm?"

I repeated what I had said, slower and a bit louder.

Again, he said, "Hmm, I no understand."

I perceived him to be an intelligent person, but I also immediately realized that he was faking.

I asked, "What language do you speak? Where are you from?"

I could tell he understood what I said, yet he pretended otherwise.

He mumbled, "I... Estonia... Russian army... we speak Russia."

I asked in fluent Russian, *"Wy goworitje po ruskiy?"* ("Do you speak Russian?")

He continued mumbling, "In war... I live Germany... we speak Germany."

In perfect German, I asked, *"Sprechen Sie deutsch?"* ("Do you speak German?")

The moment I asked that question, he picked up a flowerpot, held it high between his face and mine, and said in perfect English, "Does your wife like flowers?" I decided to stop tormenting him any further. I took the flowers and went home. Each time I share this story with someone, we have a good laugh.

When I planned to build our house, I decided to make it large enough for a family, not just for the two of us. With this in mind, I decided to build a storey and a half, with two bedrooms on the main floor and two on the second level. Considering our future needs, I decided to rough in the plumbing in a large walk-in closet on

Our house on Gregory Road

the upper floor to allow for a second washroom when needed. It turned out to be the right thing to do.

Whenever a new baby arrived, we kept him on the main floor in the second bedroom close to our bedroom, which also served as my office. Once the boys grew a little older, I finished the upper washroom and put two boys in each upstairs bedroom. Since I was a practical and economical person, I did all the finish carpentry myself, while Kaethe helped with the staining and painting. However, we left the walls and ceilings on both levels unpainted with plain, white plaster.

Both levels were heated, but we had no air conditioning. On many hot summer nights, I found it difficult to sleep. I was tired before I left home for work. One day in 1962, I decided we needed air conditioning. Other people installed swimming pools in their backyard for $5,000 or more to cool off. Central air conditioning would cost a mere $800.

We soon installed a two-ton unit to keep our whole house comfortable. Knowing that the upper bedrooms became even warmer in the summer than the ones on the main floor, I had the contractor install additional ducts for the children's rooms. This unit lasted for more than thirty-five years. We finally replaced it just a few years ago. I will never forget waking up that first morning after sleeping in an air-conditioned room; I was refreshed and ready to take on the world!

We had a large playroom in the basement. In addition to buying appropriate toys for our boys, I also made different types of wooden blocks. Some of them were shaped like small bricks. It amazed me that they preferred the blocks to the fancy toys. Years later, those blocks with square edges had worn totally round.

As they became older, we bought tricycles, bicycles, and many other things to keep them occupied and have fun with. I even built a large swing for them outdoors, like my father made for us in Russia, which held four or five children at the same time.

Walter and Helmut playing with the blocks I made for them.

Peter with another type of building blocks I made.

One day I saw a contraption—either on television or in a magazine—and decided to make one for the boys. I fastened one end of a ten-metre cable to the basement wall close to the ceiling and the other about a metre lower on the opposite wall. I attached a seat with a pulley, so the boys could slide down on it. Not only did our boys enjoy it, but so did the other neighbourhood kids. A few years ago, one of our neighbours, who now had children of his own, asked me about the cable slide he had used as a small boy.

We always had children around our house, especially during the days when Kaethe was home alone. She enjoyed baking for them, and they loved to eat. One day one of the children commented, "Mrs. Braun, you are the best baker in the whole wide world!"

This was also an opportunity for Kaethe to influence the neighbourhood children in a positive way. Once a week through the winter, we had Child Evangelism at our home. In summer we held Vacation Bible School in our backyard. We had quite a number of children attend these meetings. Although Kaethe was a teacher, she was relatively new in Canada and didn't feel comfortable teaching in English. Therefore, we had other young women, including Helene Boldt, come and teach the classes.

This ministry bore fruit, as two of our children received Jesus as their Saviour. I don't know how many of the neighbour children made that decision, but we did learn about one in the 1980s. Larry Shantz, the Pastor of Bethany Community Church, came to tell us that one of his church members had become a Christian in our Bible classes. He came to thank and encourage us. We have been members of his church for many years. Our other two sons also made that important decision later on—the best decision of a lifetime.

Swinging with Peter on my lap; Walter (facing camera) and a neighbourhood boy on the big swing.

CHAPTER 24

Fun with Our Children

Even though I worked during the day and had paperwork to do in the evening, I still took time to play with our children. I loved to play tricks with them. When their hands became cold from making snowballs, I'd say, "Let's warm up this snowball with some warm water." I'll never forget the look on their faces as it slowly disappeared!

One night we drove home in the moonlight. There was a half-moon on this particular night. One of the younger boys asked, "Why is the moon broken?"

Jokingly, I said, "Daddy will fix it."

One of the older boys repeated what I had just said in a childlike, comforting tone, "Daddy will fix it." While it was never my habit to lie to them, I always loved to have fun with them.

In the summer, we played games on the lawn or went for walks along the street or to the lake close by. I told them stories my mother had told me when I was a young boy. We went for car rides and showed them every possible sight we could think of. Whenever we had a particularly beautiful snowfall, we all jumped into the car and drove around to admire the scenery and take pictures of the snow-laden trees and shrubs.

We also loved to skate on the Fifteen Mile Creek, which was just across the street. When the boys were small, I skated with them in my arms. Once they were bigger, we bought them skates.

After a heavy snowfall, we played in the snow. We threw snowballs and jumped in deep drifts. One of the boys usually ended up completely buried in the snow.

Another sport I always loved is hunting. I purchased a shotgun and took the family out hunting. The boys loved it! I don't remember ever coming home with a lot of "game," but we had fun trekking through the forest, taking aim and banging at something flying in the air.

I wasn't much of a fisherman, although I loved camping. On one occasion, I took Sieg and Peter on a trip up north. We rented a boat and fishing tackle and set out to catch some fish. Unfortunately, we didn't have much success until the last few minutes. When we finally made a catch, Sieg squealed, "If this is how it works…!" This became supper for the three of us.

All four of the boys used to wrestle with me on the living room carpet. After a while, I allowed them to hold me down on the floor, with all of them on top of me. They thought it was hilarious, especially when I yelled, "Mom! Mom! Come! Help me! Help! Help!"

Christmas time was always special, of course, as it is for all children. When I grew up in the former Soviet Union, we couldn't expect much. We often had next to nothing to eat—never mind toys. However, our parents did what they could. At times, we received gifts such as gloves, a scarf, or a pair of new socks. We also received *some* toys most years. We had some beautiful English bone china, which was probably inherited from my father's parents. On Christmas Eve, we each picked out one of these very special porcelain plates to set on the table to be filled with our gifts by the next morning. We woke up long before daybreak with much excitement to look at them.

For my own children, I woke up early and started playing Christmas carols on the piano. As soon as they heard the music, all four of them jumped out of bed with lightning speed and dressed in a *big* hurry. When I started to play *"Ihr Kindelein kommet,"* ("Come hither, ye children,") eight little feet came rumbling down the stairs. What a time we had opening all the gifts!

Walter on the telephone and Helmut on the tricycle

All the "men" preparing for a new lawn.

Painting the house gable; each does what he can.

Sieg on top of the world as I trimmed the tree.

CHAPTER 25

Reunion with My Mother and Siblings

When Kaethe and I think back on how we grew up, we believe every day in a country like Canada should be a special day for all of us. We have so much!

When we first married, we didn't have the interior walls painted or wallpapered, nor did we have much jewellery or many fancy gadgets. However, when it came to food on the table, we never bought anything less than the best. Kaethe and I believed it was more important to keep the children warm, dry, and well fed than to have painted walls and fancy carpets. Besides, I was the only breadwinner in the family.

We also believed in helping those in need. I especially wanted to assist my parents and seven siblings. I had lost contact with them in 1944 and had no idea where they were, or even if they were still alive.

In 1950, I received notice of their whereabouts. They had been exiled in 1945 to Swerdlowsk, in Siberia, east of the Ural Mountains. Here they suffered *unbelievable* hardships. When I found out they were living there, I knew they would be suffering—possibly even starving to death. Many of our people did actually die of hunger and frost. They lived under appalling conditions in wooden shacks. They had no heating material except what they could gather in the forest. They weren't allowed to cut down any trees; they could only pick up small branches. Besides, it would have been difficult to find a lot of heating material under the deep Siberian snow.

I started to correspond with them. From time to time, I offered to help them, but they declined with thanks. I believed their situation was the same as it had been in the 1930s. The last thing I wanted to do was make life even more difficult for them.

When I lived with my family in Russia in the 1930s, we corresponded with our relatives in Canada. They sent us food parcels until the political situation became too tense between the Communist and Capitalist states. Because it became so risky, my parents simply quit writing to my mother's sisters in Canada. Any contact with other countries could have been interpreted as treason to the Soviet State. I had no reason to believe this had changed after the war.

Finally, in 1962, we purchased a new car for the first time. Since we had been corresponding freely with my family for some time, we included a photo of our new 1963 Pontiac in one of our letters. Shortly after that, one of my sisters wrote and commented on our new car. Evidently, mother had said, "If they're living this well, they might want to send us something." We had been waiting for this hint for a long time! They had not held back for political reasons; they were simply too modest to ask for help.

We didn't waste any time. We sent them parcels for many years, until things finally improved for them. We sent materials for making clothes and expensive blankets, which they could sell for a good price, then buy food with the money. We were never rich, but the Lord blessed us with good health and enough work to be able to give to others.

I appreciated how Kaethe always supported me in helping my family. She never complained about spending hundreds of dollars to help her in-laws, even when we often had to pay more for postage than for what the parcel contained. Someone told us only a small part of the cost was for postage; the Communists used the rest to finance Soviet spies in the free world. We had no control over that. We tried to overlook this when we realized how much our parcels helped our family. They often expressed their gratitude for the help we sent. They told me they often thanked God for sending a "Joseph" ahead, as they put it, to help them in their time of need.

Shortly before the end of the war, while still in Germany, my father had returned home and reunited with the rest of the family, except me. My youngest brother Hans told me that the German military had demanded that Father join the German S.S. troops. Since he was a Christian and firmly believed it was wrong to kill, he refused to join. Finally, they threatened him to either join or be hanged the next day. Hans told us how father had wrestled all night long with the Lord, quoting one scripture verse after another. The next day, the American Army conquered and occupied that area. God had answered his prayer!

During the Khrushchev years, we finally heard that some of our people had received permission to leave the Soviet Union and immigrate to Canada. Of course, it had always been my hope and vision to see all of my family again. Unfortunately, this was not to be. I will never forget the day we received the news that my father had passed away on September 28, 1971, at the age of sixty-eight. While some people believe it's not proper for men to cry, I certainly did upon hearing that news. I felt great disappointment and a deep pain in my heart. I know he is in heaven, where we will have an even greater family reunion one day.

It was indeed a time of rejoicing and celebration when the Communists finally allowed families to reunite. In 1978, my youngest brother Hans and his family finally emigrated from Russia to Germany. We had not seen one another for thirty-three years. He was seven years old when I last saw him in 1944; now he was forty, married, and had children. After he arrived in Germany, he contacted us via telephone. Not long after that, he came to visit us in Canada. When he called us to be picked up from the airport in Toronto, we wasted no time picking him up and bringing him to our home.

He mentioned that he had brought along the name, address, and telephone number of one of his friends who lived in St. Catharines. In the event we weren't interested in seeing him, he would contact them and stay with them. Well, that sounded ridiculous! There was nothing we wanted more than to see and to embrace a member of my family who I had missed for so many years. What a celebration we had!

I am so fortunate that my dear wife Kaethe loves all of my family. She has a soft heart and was the first to weep with joy upon meeting them. And you'd better believe it was contagious.

Soon other family members came to Germany. Kaethe and I went to visit them. On one of our visits, three of my brothers picked us up from the railroad station in Bielefeld. This was the first time I had met all of my brothers since they came out of Russia. It was a reunion we had all looked forward to. We gave and received a lot of hugs and warm embraces from all their families. It truly was a time of celebration and giving thanks to God.

When I said goodbye to my mother on December 15, 1944, at a railroad station in Poland, I don't recall it being an exceptionally emotional experience. Neither do I recall specifically what she said. We didn't know what awaited us the next day or even the next hour. However, I do recall that she gave me a Bible verse to remember before we left the house: *"Trust in the Lord with all your heart and do not lean on your own understanding. In all your ways acknowledge Him, and He will make your paths straight"* (Proverbs 3:5–6).

My dear mother finally arrived in Germany in 1980. We wasted no time booking a flight there, as we had done many times. However, this was a special reunion. I can't think of a better way to express what this visit with Mother and my family was like than to remind you of the story of the reunion of Joseph with his brothers:

> Then Joseph could not control himself before all those who stood by him, and he cried, "Have everyone go out from me." So there was no man with him when Joseph made himself known to his brothers. He wept so loudly that the Egyptians heard it, and the household of Pharaoh heard of it. (Genesis 45:1–2)

My family in Germany in 1980.
Front: Susanna, Margarete, Mother, Liese & Tina.
Back: Jake, Franz, Peter & Hans.

Now you know what it was like to see my mother after all those thirty-six years of separation!

In 1981, Mother came to visit us in Canada with her grandson Johann. It was the first opportunity for all our sons to meet their Oma. It would also be their last, except for Helmut, who visited her once in Germany. She was also able to meet Tina, one of her three sisters who had immigrated to Canada in the 1920s. She had not seen any of them for fifty-six years. Unfortunately, her oldest sister Liese had already passed away and her youngest sister Anna lived too far away, in Manitoba, to join us.

The last time we visited Mother in Germany, she didn't recognize us anymore. Her face was still friendly and sweet, especially when her granddaughter Rita came into her room with a baby in her arms. In 1990, after we had returned home from our vacation, my brother Hans called us and told us that Mother's last hours had been difficult. Finally, Hans had suggested, "Let's pray and sing her favourite song."

Suddenly, she stopped labouring. With heavenly glory and a smile on her face, she peacefully slipped away to be with Jesus.

CHAPTER 26

Our Trips

I had an insatiable desire to learn more about the world I lived in. I decided to travel; I wanted to see the world. Since I made that decision, I have seen a good part of it. I travelled little when I was single, because my first priority was to build a house, get married, and have a family. After reaching that goal, Kaethe and I travelled together. When our children were toddlers, we would leave them with either Grandma or another dependable person.

On our first trip, we went to Ottawa, the capital of Canada. We visited Thousand Islands and the famous Boldt Castle. In 1965, we went to New York City to the World Fair. What an unforgettable experience that was! I saw countless fascinating pavilions with some of the most incredible inventions and demonstrations; it almost

At Thousand Islands in 1967 with Helmut and Walter.

blew me away! While we visited the Big Apple, we seized the opportunity to see some of the world's tallest structures—the Empire State building, the Rockefeller Centre, the United Nations, Radio City Music Hall, and much more. When the boys became a bit older, we took them with us to New York, Washington, and many other places in the United States.

In 1967, we took nine-year-old Helmut and eight-year-old Walter to the World Fair in Montreal. The fair was outstanding! I could write a book about it. We continued our trip all the way through New Brunswick and Prince Edward Island. We also stopped at Magnetic Hill. When we put our vehicle in neutral, it appeared to roll uphill.

*On top of the Rockefeller Centre looking
towards the Empire State Building.*

A family trip stopover in Washington, DC.

Helmut and Walter feeding a chipmunk.

Helmut and Walter camping in Northern Ontario.

For the night, we slept in my homemade camper; on other trips, before we had a camper, we used a tent. Sometimes at our camping site, chipmunks scrambled up onto the boys' laps as they fed them. They always enjoyed this. As soon as Peter was old enough to come along, our whole family went camping in northern Ontario.

The homemade camper was my own invention. I built a top for my half-ton pickup—actually, it was a telescopic unit. By turning a crank, the outside wall with the roof could be raised high enough for an adult to stand upright. I constructed a six-by-six-foot space over the cab. When the roof was in the down position, this space was about twelve inches high; in the up position, it was at least twenty-four inches, high enough for the four boys to sleep comfortably. On the bottom, I arranged a sleeping area for the two of us. During the day, we converted it into an eating area.

We always travelled with it in the down position for less wind resistance, more stability, and better fuel economy. Wherever we stopped at a campsite, people questioned me about the unit; some even offered to buy it. Since it was so unique, it was easily recognizable. On our way home from a six-week trip out West, we stopped at a fuelling station in Chicago where someone came over to us and said, "I saw you in San Francisco!"

Our homemade camper in the up position on our 1968 trip out west.

Our improved second camper.

Several people suggested I patent the camper. I actually went to an agent to inquire about it. He encouraged me to do so. However, when I began to realize the amount of "red tape" involved, I became discouraged and didn't pursue it any further. About two years later, I saw several campers built like mine. Someone must have liked the idea and was more willing than I to get it patented.

In 1968, we traveled west through Canada to Victoria on Vancouver Island. Then we drove south to Los Angeles. It turned out to be a six-week trip.

One of the highlights was visiting my mother's youngest sister Anna and her husband, Henry Epp, in Steinbach, Manitoba. We also saw the Mennonite Museum there. We stayed in Winnipeg for a short time to visit friends I knew from Russia, as well as Kaethe's relatives from Paraguay.

Shortly after we arrived at the home of Kaethe's niece Elsie, four-year-old Peter caught sight of a tricycle and took off to inspect the neighbourhood. Because we were busy visiting with the relatives, some of whom we had never met before, Kaethe and I didn't see him leave. All of a sudden, we noticed that Peter was missing! We searched everywhere, but he was nowhere in sight. We called, but no answer came. In desperation, we finally called the police. Fortunately, someone in the

*My mother's sister, Aunt Anna, and Uncle Epp in
Steinbach, Manitoba, 1968.*

neighbourhood had seen him cross a heavily-travelled road, picked him up, and brought him safely back to us. We experienced a small taste of the desperation parents feel when a child goes missing. We certainly did a lot of praying and crying out to the Lord!

From there, we drove through the prairies and on through Alberta and British Columbia, where we saw the Rocky Mountains for the first time. I had studied about these in geography class, but now I saw them with my own eyes. Someone commented that the mountains were so high they touched the sky. As we ascended one of the highest peaks on a lift three miles long, Peter stretched out his hand as high as he could and, with face beaming, he exclaimed, "I'm touching the sky!"

In Vancouver, we found many old acquaintances from my home village in the Ukraine. It was humbling to hear so many positive comments about my parents. Kaethe was deeply touched to become acquainted with these dear in-laws whom she had never met.

On top of the Rocky Mountains where Peter touched the sky.

From Vancouver, we boarded a ferry to Vancouver Island and toured the city of Victoria. We saw Butchart Gardens and the Undersea Aquarium before driving north to Port Alberni. We went to a provincial park there that has the largest and tallest Douglas fir trees anywhere in the world. They were, indeed, monstrosities! Our family of six stood around one of these trees, each touching the fingertips of the other to see if we could reach around it. Afterwards, I measured the rest of the distance and found it would have required two more adults to reach all the way around. Amazing!

From there, we crossed the border and stopped in Seattle, Washington, to see the Space Needle, built for the 1962 World Fair. Of course, we all went to the top of this marvellous piece of architecture. I was awestricken!

We continued south through Oregon and into California. I expected it to be hot there, especially in the summer. However, when we arrived in Crescent City, it seemed cool in the evening. As we continued further south to San Francisco to see the Golden Gate Bridge, we stood there shivering, even though we wore winter coats.

The sight of the city was unforgettable on that bright, sunny day. The white buildings glistened in magnificence and splendour. It reminded me of the description of the heavenly Jerusalem in the Book of Revelation.

We went to see the world's oldest trees, the Sequoia Redwoods. It was worthwhile going all the way to California just to see those giants. The largest of them was named "General Sherman." It measured twenty-eight metres in circumference at one metre from the ground.

Some trees, even with living branches and green foliage, had a tunnel chopped through them so that cars could drive through. I saw a piece of bark from one of the trees measuring forty centimetres thick.

We crossed the Golden Gate Bridge on our way to Reedley to visit Kaethe's Uncle Henry and his family. The weather was hot. They offered us a refreshing shower; then we spent the night in our camper on their driveway. We also visited one of my best friends, Hans Kasdorf, and his family in Fresno.

Visiting Hans Kasdorfs in Fresno, California.

As we went further south, it became even warmer. When we first arrived in Los Angeles, we stopped and asked a service station attendant how far it was to

Disneyland. He said, "It's fifty miles from here." I could hardly believe it was still that far away.

"You're telling me we're in the city of Los Angeles, and it's another fifty miles to Disneyland?" I asked.

He advised us to stay there overnight and leave early in the morning. Otherwise, it would take three to four hours to get there in traffic, instead of forty-five minutes. We followed his advice. We, and especially the boys, enjoyed our visit to Disneyland.

After being away from home for about four weeks, we started to slowly wend our way back to Canada. When Peter heard the words "going home," he immediately protested: "No, I don't want to go home!" From then on, we only told him the name of the next city or park.

We decided to go through Yellowstone National Park in Wyoming on our return trip. What a worthwhile place to spend some time with all its lakes, ponds, boiling water, colourful streams, canyon, and waterfalls. Old Faithful spewed boiling water high into the air at such accurate intervals that we could set our clock by it.

We found a wonderful bakery in a German colony in Iowa where they baked bread in old-fashioned ovens. The fragrance of the freshly baked bread was mouthwatering. It tasted as good as Mother's bread, which she had made in our brick oven in the Ukraine.

From there, we drove towards Chicago. I wanted to see the Marina Twin Towers, which I had read about in Reader's Digest. We rode up the elevator to see the view from the top. The Science Centre in this midwestern city was another fascinating place to visit. After viewing many interesting exhibits, a security officer directed us to a certain piece of art by Picasso. It was a huge metal statue about eight metres tall. Part of it resembled a horse, part a guitar, and part an angel.

Our boys at Yellowstone National Park.

"What's this supposed to represent?" I asked.

"I don't know, either," he replied. "But everyone wants to see it and take pictures."

Before we left Chicago, we stopped at a market with dozens of stalls with huge watermelons; the price was $3 each. Oh, they were mighty good! With this, our trip had nearly ended. It was a time well spent with the family. Even though I could have stayed home in the summertime and made good money, we believed spending time with the family and seeing the wonderful world God had made was even more important.

For years, we spent several weeks in Florida each winter. We visited all the places of interest—Disneyworld, the Sunken Gardens, Miami, Key West, the Coral Reefs, and the Kennedy Space Centre. Some years, we went with all four of our sons; other years, the older two stayed home.

Picking and eating oranges for the first time in Florida.

On January 28, 1986, Kaethe and I had tickets to see the space shuttle blast off. Tragically, this happened to be the Challenger; it blew up in front of our eyes less than two minutes after launching. It was truly unforgettable to watch the space shuttle take off, but our excitement soon turned to horror.

In 1980, someone told us about a Christian conference centre south of Tampa, near Bradenton, Florida. It had hotels, motels, campgrounds, and a tabernacle with daily Christian services. This place had palm trees, orange trees, and many different shrubs and flowers. They also had a swimming pool and outdoor games, such as shuffleboard and horseshoes.

One day, Kaethe and I decided to locate this place and camp there for a few weeks. We did find it and spent several weeks there for many winters; we enjoyed it immensely. On one of our trips to Florida, Sieg and Peter, who were in their teens, wanted to come along, but not to the Christian retreat. They wanted to camp by themselves at Apopka, north of Orlando, where we had camped with them before. It meant taking along a tent and all their extra camping gear. Kaethe and I agreed. We dropped them off at this beautiful place with a crystal clear spring-fed creek nearby. Then we continued on our way to the conference centre at Bradenton.

After about a week, Kaethe and I decided to visit our sons and see how they were doing at Apopka, about a four-hour drive away. We will never forget the way they welcomed us; they were more than ready to come with us! We packed up and returned to Bradenton. The boys soon fell in love with this location.

Some years later, they came along again. This time, Sieg was seventeen. One evening after we came back from the tabernacle to our campsite, he said he wanted to go back and participate in some program with the other young people. I had a sneaking suspicion something was up and jokingly asked, "Are you going deer hunting?"

When he returned without much enthusiasm, I asked, "How was your hunting trip? Did you find any deer?"

"No, just goats!" he grunted.

We have often been surprised that they both came along with us at their age.

In 1984, Kaethe and I decided to visit Hawaii. Our youngest son Peter was studying on the Big Island with Youth with a Mission (YWAM). We decided to visit four of the main islands. We travelled by train to Vancouver and flew to Honolulu. The snow-covered trees and surrounding scenery on the train trip in winter were outstanding and unforgettable!

Hawaii had fascinated me all of my life; now I saw it with my own eyes—huge ocean waves, pineapples growing in the fields, hot boiling steam coming out of the earth, and huge black lava fields on the Big Island. We saw the uniquely shaped mountains, the rainbows on the island of Kauai, and the huge Banyan trees on Maui. It was indescribable!

One day the tour guide told us about the Kukui nut. He explained how oily it was and said, "If you're constipated, eat one of these nuts and you'll be just fine. If you eat two of them, you'll have to rush. If you eat three or more, don't even try it. You'll never make it!"

We spent part of the time with Peter. We rented a car and took him with us to see the interesting sights on the Big Island, where he studied. We stayed at the YWAM campus for a few nights. They welcomed us and treated us like royalty.

Sieg lived in Calgary at the time of our Hawaii trip. Before we left St. Catharines by train for Vancouver, we arranged with him to meet us at the railroad station in Calgary, then accompany us to Vancouver, where he planned to spend some time with Kaethe's relatives. At first, he didn't want to take time off from work. Then he became excited about it and came along with us. The three of us had a wonderful time together.

In the early 1990s, I received about $2,000 from the German government to repay us for part of the loss of our home and possessions in the Ukraine. One day I offered Peter to take a trip with me to my former home in Russia using the money I had received. A few years passed before he responded. One day he asked me, "Is your offer to go to Russia still valid?" I assured him that it was.

In 1998, he made all the flight and hotel arrangements. My responsibility was to brush up on the Russian language. I borrowed books and tapes from the library and started to polish my Russian.

Kaethe and I thought it would be a good idea to make a stopover in Germany and visit my relatives who resided there now. At first Peter didn't seem to have much interest in doing that. However, Kaethe encouraged him not to let this opportunity slip by. After giving it some thought, he agreed. We first flew to Frankfurt, Germany. My relatives picked us up from the airport. Peter had his first opportunity to visit most of my relatives—most, not *all* of them—because over two hundred of them were scattered around the country. He made friends with many of them in a short time. One day he said, "They're really a great bunch of people!"

From Frankfurt, we flew to Kiev, the Ukrainian capital. Peter had arranged to stay at a missionary centre for two days. The young man who picked us up at the airport spoke limited English. The condition of the vehicle we were riding in was such that, in the western world, it would have been sent to the wreckers. The highway to the centre was rougher than I had seen anywhere else. The car rattled, shook, and smoked as he zipped along at 120 kilometers per hour. I was greatly relieved when we reached our destination.

Peter and I visiting the village where I grew up.

Several days later, we took a twelve-hour trip by train to Zaporozhye, thirty kilometres from my hometown. Arriving there seemed like a miracle! A young German-speaking man in his forties picked us up at the railroad station and took us to one of his church member's home for the next two nights. Before he left, he told us he would pick us up the next morning and take us all day wherever we wanted to go. We couldn't have wished for more.

The family we stayed with for those two nights spoke neither German nor English. Whatever Russian

The plot of land where our house used to stand.

Peter and I at my father's former carpentry shop.

I still remembered came in handy. The young minister returned the next day as he had promised and took us to my hometown, where I had spent the first sixteen years of my life. What an unforgettable experience! Unfortunately, our house was not there anymore. There was only a small heap of rubble—probably from the walls of the house. The lot was full of weeds.

Peter and I took with us a few stones and a bit of soil from my former home. It was an emotional experience to once more see and stand on the ground where I had been born, grown up, gone to school, worked, and had so much fun. I truly felt at home, in spite of the fact that my family had gone through many rough times there.

I visited the place where my father had worked for many years, the school I used to go to, the village store, and other places that interested me. I met an elderly Russian lady who had refused to go along with the others to Germany in 1943. She was the former wife of one of our Mennonites. I knew she used to speak *Plautdittsch*, so I asked her to say something in this Low German dialect. However, she refused, except to say three words: *"Aunton Dicklje Tina,"* the name of her former friend Tina Dueck, who had left with the others for Germany.

On the second day, another young man picked us up and took us to other places of interest, and to several stores to do some shopping. We saw some interesting sights and made new friends. We realized how privileged we are in the western world in comparison to this country.

On the return trip, we returned to Frankfurt, where everything seemed to be as different as day and night from what we had seen in the Ukraine. The floors at the airport were sparkling clean with a shiny finish on them. The Autobahn was smooth riding. Peter jokingly asked, "Where are all the holes in the road?" After visiting more friends and relatives, we flew home to Toronto, where Kaethe, Peter's wife Kathy, and their daughter Jessica met us.

In 2009, we invited Sieg and Karen to come with us to visit all their many uncles, aunts, and cousins in Germany. They both agreed to come along. Karen had said, "If my father-in-law is paying, who wouldn't go?" We booked a flight to Frankfurt for June 16, 2009. While Sieg and Karen could only go for a week, Kaethe and I went for two.

It was a joy for us to see how quickly Sieg and Karen connected with these relatives they had never seen, especially since Karen didn't speak German. Fortunately, many of the young people in Germany speak fluent English. Almost all of my siblings with their children and grandchildren live in Germany.

Ernest Regehr, one of my nephews, picked us up from the airport in Frankfurt. We cruised along the Autobahn at about 180 kilometres per hour to his home 120 kilometres from the airport. One day, Ernest gave us a tour of the factory where he was a foreman. It produced paper napkins and other paper products. He explained the different functions of many machines and materials used in the factory. We even had the opportunity to meet the owner of the factory. He and his daughter spoke perfect English.

Sieg and Karen stayed at Ernest and Irene's place for part of the time. One day Ernest and Irene took them via train to the city of Colon on the Rhine River. They visited the famous Cathedral, the Koelner Dom, and many other places. Karen was amazed at how fast the trains moved along the rails, especially when one of them met another going the opposite direction.

Towards the end of their stay in Germany, Sieg said he had planned to rent a car to go sightseeing, but he didn't need to after his cousins had taken them everywhere. They even talked about going for another visit to Germany sometime in the future.

We enjoyed singing and making music with our relatives there. Kaethe especially loves music and was deeply touched as she joined them in singing with all their hearts. All of a sudden, Karen handed me a Kleenex without saying a word. I knew the reason, of course. I passed it on to Kaethe, who had good reason to use it. After wiping her tears, she asked where I had gotten it. I said, "From your daughter-in-law." Yes, the two of them love one another and get along well.

My family in Germany
Front: Susanna, Mother, Margarete
Back: Franz and Helena, Luise and Cornelius, Tina and Victor,
Liese and Peter, Kaethe and Jake, Rita and Johann

One day in 2010, Kaethe and I were watching television when we saw the new government building Reichstag in Berlin. I told Kaethe we had to see that someday. Besides Berlin, I also wanted to see London and Paris. As I was dreaming about that, I saw myself riding at 300 kilometres per hour on the Euro-rail through the English Chunnel from London to Paris. However, at the age of eighty-two, I had to confess that I wasn't interested in making the arrangements with all the complexities of this high-tech world. I had an idea; I knew Peter loved to travel as much as his father. Besides that, he liked to make travel arrangements for other people. Before long, we asked him about it, offering to take both him and Kathy, as well as Walter, with us. Walter declined the offer; Kathy also decided to stay home with the children. Peter made all the arrangements and we flew from Toronto to London.

We visited St. Paul's Cathedral and the Bloody Mary museum, with all the exhibits from the British Royalty, including the Royal Crown. After several days, we left for Paris via Euro-rail. We took a city bus tour and a tour on the River Seine. We went to see the Eiffel Tower and the spectacular palace of Louis XIV in Versailles.

From there, we returned by rail to Germany where we visited some of my relatives. It was a joy to hear Peter communicating with his cousins, uncles, and aunts in fluent German, and sometimes even joking in

Plautdietsch. He connected with them, and they with him, like old friends.

From here, we went to Berlin. Several things impressed me in this great city. I had lived in Germany during and three years after the war, when almost every nation was an enemy to Germany. I noted with particular interest that a British man had designed the Reichstag. Not far from there stood a Jewish Synagogue with a golden dome. In another part of the city we saw a huge Jewish cemetery with thousands of gravestones — a memorial of the Holocaust. On the bus tour, the driver drew our attention to a large building named "Jimmy Carter's Smile," donated by the United States. It was so touching; I almost started to sob.

We now have an empty nest and can travel wherever we like. We usually visit Peter and his family in Charlotte, North Carolina, twice every year. We often go to Germany to visit my family and friends, and some of Kaethe's. We have visited the Drehers, the family where I stayed after the war, several times. We feel so blessed to have travelled the world.

The Dreher family who invited me to live with them after I was released from the POW camp. Front: Mother Dreher. Back: Otto, Elfriede and Helmut.

CHAPTER 27

Final Reflections

Many things began to interest me early on in life. Science and technology have always fascinated me. How can a whistle create a sound? How does a guitar string create a different pitch by tightening and loosening the strings? How does electricity move along a wire? How does a steam engine work? How can a train ride along such narrow tracks and not slip off? Long before I had ever seen a train on a railroad track, other than from pictures or someone telling me about them, I tried to figure out in my mind how it could ride on such narrow tracks. All of a sudden, it occurred to me—the wheels must have a lip on either the inside or the outside. Sure enough! When I saw a train for the first time, I found it to be so.

I wanted to know how a mirror clearly reflects an image. Any one I had ever seen had either black or red paint on the back of it. One day, I tried to make one with one of our neighbour's boys. We brushed some red paint on the back of a piece of glass, but it didn't reflect. Thomas Edison allegedly said, "I have not failed. I have just found 10,000 ways that won't work." We found one way *not* to make a mirror.

Why can you set paper on fire by directing sunlight through a magnifying glass? Why is the sun so much larger at sunrise and sunset than during the day? Why does the sunset appear golden sometimes and bright red at other times? Someone told me I could predict the next day's weather by the different colours of the evening sky. I began to forecast; actually I became quite good at it!

I wanted to know more about our solar system and our galaxy, the Milky Way. Much later, in the 1950s, I bought several books and borrowed others. According to a report I read on the Internet recently, the Hubble Space Telescope has determined that there are 125 billion galaxies in the universe; each of the galaxies has two hundred to four hundred billion stars. Incomprehensible!

When I was in my twenties, I became deeply interested in psychology. I always found it interesting to observe people and felt I had the ability to tell if a person was telling the truth or not. I read every article I could find on this subject. One day I found a large psychology book in a bookstore. Before I bought it, I consulted an elderly minister about it. He said, "Psychology is a controversial subject. It's difficult to evaluate and can be misleading." After hearing this, I gave up on this book. Many years later, I realized how damaging and destructive the application of ungodly psychology can be!

Space travel has always fascinated me. I heard talk about flying to the planet Mars when I was a young boy in Russia. Decades later, when several nations became serious about space travel and going to the moon, some Christian leaders and preachers interpreted this idea as blasphemy—even like declaring war against the Creator. One of my most respected ministers preached boldly that such an idea was pure nonsense. He added, "It will never happen!" Then he quoted many verses, including Genesis 1:28— *"Subdue the earth"* —and added, "Not the moon!"

As time passed, it became more and more likely that scientists and engineers would actually be able to accomplish this great feat. This minister changed his position somewhat and said from the pulpit, "Men might go to the moon, but if they do, they will never return to earth." Years later, after the first astronauts had actually landed on the moon and returned safely to the earth, he said, "I always knew they would."

Our church also taught that watching television was inappropriate for Christians. However, when I found out rockets had been launched into space, I could no longer resist. In 1959, we purchased our first black-and-white television.

I was gullible when I was young, but when I became aware of many foolish statements, prophecies and predictions, including those I shared above, I decided no longer to follow a leader blindly. When challenged on one occasion, after many false accusations, I stood my ground and said in front of more than twenty church leaders, "As for me, it has once and for all become history to accept anything from anyone without using my own evaluation and checking Scripture."

While I haven't acquired a high degree of education, I do feel blessed to have an interest in many areas. I loved good music, but I didn't aim to become famous. I played the piano and organ in a large church for a number of years. Kaethe and I now serve in several senior citizen homes; she sings and I play the instrument. People have expressed appreciation for this service. What a blessing it is to be involved in the lives of others!

After retiring, I pursued my interest in finer wood-working and have done a lot of wood turning. I'm amazed at the multitude of different kinds of wood on the planet. I have personally used more than sixty-five varieties. Every piece has its own particular beauty, but some exotic woods are extraordinary—amazing in colour and grain. I have made wooden bowls, candle holders, pencil holders, containers with and without a lid, pepper mills, salt shakers, lighthouses, and countless other things.

One of my jewellery boxes.

I sold many of these items at craft shows. It's so rewarding to hear people express awe and amazement at the uniqueness and beauty of the wood, as well as the craftsmanship. Even other wood turners ask me for advice about certain techniques. Some of them came to my shop to learn. I also had to learn from others. George Enns, one of my former employees in finish carpentry and an outstanding artistic wood turner, taught me a lot about how to use the lathe.

Some examples of my woodturning.

When our sons reached the age of sixteen, I believed it would be a good experience for them to take a year off from school and work with me in finish carpentry. I received criticism for that decision. One of Kaethe's uncles, a well-to-do farmer with a large family and a respected member in his church, did the same. All of his children turned out well—finished their education

One of the many cabinets I made.

and found employment later. Two of our sons, Walter and Sieg, make their living in woodworking. Peter performed quite well in carpentry, but never became too excited about it.

Peter liked electronic gadgets. He tried to get me excited about a computer, but I had no time for it, since I was still fully occupied with my trade. I told him, "Peter, I don't know how to set my digital watch. What do you want me to do with a computer?"

Of course, he wanted one, but didn't have the money to buy one. He kept insisting, "My friend's fathers have computers. If they can learn, you can, too."

Finally I said, "Peter, I need a computer like you need a table saw!" With this, he left me in peace for several years.

However, after he married and his children had started to read and write, he and Kathy insisted once again that I buy a computer. I heard them say that their other Grandpa was writing them e-mails. "It takes way too long to get your snail mail," they told me.

In April of 2003, I finally purchased one. A retired couple came to our house every week for quite a while to teach me. Now I feel quite comfortable with anything that has to do with e-mail and searching the Internet.

My "Digital Ensemble."

A few years ago, I purchased a wonderful instrument called a digital ensemble. It has eighty-eight keys, like a piano. With this one instrument, I can simulate the music of up to 150 different instruments. I can play six different organs, four pianos, and even two instruments at the same time. I can record music and play it back. The quality of the sound is most impressive. When I play one of the mighty cathedral organs combined with another instrument, it sounds like the real thing! Because I usually practice for performing in the senior's homes, our house is often filled with music. I never get tired of it.

Another thing I enjoy is good, clean humour. Ecclesiastes 3:4 says, *"[There is] a time to weep and a time to laugh."* I heard a German comedian say in the 1940s, *"Lachen ist gesund."* ("Laughter is healthy.") Scientists have long promoted the benefits of it. One of them said, "If you have less than fifteen hearty laughs a day, you're undernourished on laughter."

A pastor told the following true story. A doctor informed a man that he had only six months to live. The man said, "If this is all the time I have, I want to spend it being happy." After a day full of humour, he felt better. That encouraged him to continue. To make a long story short, he was still alive after fifteen years and was doing well.

Here's another story I heard. After the war in the 1940s, during the time of Russian occupation in eastern Germany, people were hungry for lack of food. A Russian officer presented a speech in a hall filled with German citizens. He scolded them, saying, "When I listen to your conversations, all I hear is 'bread, meat, potatoes, butter, and milk.' In the Soviet Union, we talk about education, technology, science, and progress. What's the matter with you people?" An eighty-year-old woman stood up and said, *"Herr Leutnant, ein jeder spricht von dem, was er nicht hat."* ("Each one speaks about the things he doesn't have.")

A minister once illustrated a point by putting three jars on a table. He filled the first jar with alcohol, the second with tobacco smoke, and the third with clean soil. Then he put a worm into each jar. At the end of his sermon, he announced: "The worm in the jar with alcohol is dead; the one in the jar with tobacco smoke is dead; the worm in the jar with clean soil is alive and doing well. What do we learn from this object lesson?" An elderly lady raised her hand and said, "As long as you drink and smoke, you won't have any worms!"

An elderly gentleman in a senior's home became acquainted with one of the women living there. After visiting one another a few times, they fell in love. One day he asked her to marry him. She said, "Yes!" A few days later, he called her and said, "Pardon me, dear, but my mind is playing tricks on me these days. I know I asked you to marry me, but I've forgotten what you said." She replied, "I'm so glad you called. I know I said 'yes,' but I can't remember who was asking the question!"

A few years ago, our son Helmut told me he had rented an apartment in Kitchener. When the landlord informed him how much monthly rent he had to pay, he said, "Well, this is more than reasonable. I'd be glad to pay you a little more."

The landlord responded, "No, thanks. This will be fine."

After hearing this story, I said, "If I ever have an argument of this nature with someone, I'm always willing to give in and be the loser, if by so doing I can gain something."

Sometime later, Helmut said, "Dad, you made my day!"

Helmut worked for a company doing income tax returns. He once asked me if I would be interested in doing the same. I said, "Helmut, if I had to choose be-tween doing income tax returns and getting a thrashing, I'd choose the latter!"

He never asked me again.

Kaethe and I are now both in our eighties. We are so thankful for good health. Many others our age are not so fortunate. However, our physical condition is not as good today as it was several decades ago. We need to go to doctors, the lab, the drug store, and even the hospi-tal for check-ups and tests. This reminds me of a Bible verse from Ecclesiastes: *"...and the years draw near when you will say, 'I have no delight in them'"* (Ecclesiates12:1). We are thankful to the Lord, though, that we don't suffer continuous severe pain. We can still enjoy and delight in so many things.

Conclusion

As I look back over more than eighty years of life, I'm thankful for the many blessings the Lord has given me. I lived through many difficulties I didn't deserve, but God spared my life many times during those years. I went through the war without ever receiving a scratch. I barely came out of the POW starvation camp alive. I have experienced many blessings I could never have earned. The dream of my childhood to live in the free world became a reality in June of 1948. For that, I thank the Almighty with all that is in me.

We know from the book of Job that the Lord allows the enemy to torment godly people. This doesn't mean I haven't failed and made mistakes. Oh, yes, I have.

Do I have any regrets? I believe I can say with a good conscience that my goal has always been to live a life pleasing to the Lord. Have I always succeeded? Of course not, but I've made an effort to do so.

To the most important person in my life, my dear wife Kaethe, thank you for the many times you have been an encouragement to me. You faithfully stood by my side in good times and bad. I couldn't find a better way of telling you what you mean to me than to quote the following:

> An excellent wife, who can find? For her worth is far above jewels. The heart of her husband trusts in her, and he will have no lack of gain. She does him good and not evil all the days of her life… She opens her mouth in wisdom, and the teaching of kindness is on her tongue. She looks well to the ways of her household, and does not eat the bread of idleness. Her children rise up and bless her: her husband also, and he praises her, saying: "Many daughters have done nobly, but you excel them all." (Proverbs 31:10–12, 26–29)

I have shared many good and fun times in my life, as well as some deep valleys. However, I didn't take the liberty of mentioning the most difficult ones. Both Kaethe and I agree with the Apostle Paul, who said, "*We are afflicted in every way, but not crushed; perplexed, but not despairing; persecuted, but not forsaken; struck down, but not destroyed"* (2 Corinthians 4:8).

Part of an old German hymn expresses the praise in my heart:

Wenn ich, o Schoepfer, deine Macht,
die Weisheit deiner Wege,
die Liebe, die fuer Alle wacht, anbetend ueberlege:
so weiss ich, von Bewundrung voll, nicht, wie ich
Dich erheben soll.[1]

Oh Creator, when I contemplate your might
The wisdom of your ways and prayerfully consider
Your love that watches over all of us,
I am filled with amazement and admiration,
Not knowing how to lift you up and give you praise.

1   Gellert, Christian Furchtegott (1715–1769). *Wenn ich, o Schopfer, deine Macht.*

Kaethe and I on our 50th wedding anniversary.